Aboriginal Mythology

*Enthralling Myths, Legends, and Folktales
from Ancient Australia*

© Copyright 2024 - All rights reserved.

The content contained within this book may not be reproduced, duplicated, or transmitted without direct written permission from the author or the publisher.

Under no circumstances will any blame or legal responsibility be held against the publisher, or author, for any damages, reparation, or monetary loss due to the information contained within this book, either directly or indirectly.

Legal Notice:

This book is copyright protected. It is only for personal use. You cannot amend, distribute, sell, use, quote, or paraphrase any part, or the content within this book, without the consent of the author or publisher.

Disclaimer Notice:

Please note the information contained within this document is for educational and entertainment purposes only. All effort has been executed to present accurate, up-to-date, reliable, and complete information. No warranties of any kind are declared or implied. Readers acknowledge that the author is not engaging in the rendering of legal, financial, medical, or professional advice. The content within this book has been derived from various sources. Please consult a licensed professional before attempting any techniques outlined in this book.

By reading this document, the reader agrees that under no circumstances is the author responsible for any losses, direct or indirect, that are incurred as a result of the use of the information contained within this document, including, but not limited to, errors, omissions, or inaccuracies.

Free limited time bonus

Stop for a moment. We have a free bonus set up for you. The problem is this: we forget 90% of everything that we read after 7 days. Crazy fact, right? Here's the solution: we've created a printable, 1-page pdf summary for this book that you're reading now. All you have to do to get your free pdf summary is to go to the following website: https://livetolearn.lpages.co/enthrallinghistory/

Or, Scan the QR code!

Once you do, it will be intuitive. Enjoy, and thank you!

Table of Contents

INTRODUCTION 1
CHAPTER 1: DREAMTIME CREATION MYTHS 3
CHAPTER 2: SONGLINES AND THEIR SPIRITUAL SIGNIFICANCE 9
CHAPTER 3: THE LORE OF THE RAINBOW SERPENT 16
CHAPTER 4: ABORIGINAL CONSTELLATIONS AND CELESTIAL MYTHS 22
CHAPTER 5: TOTEMIC BONDS: ANIMALS AND ANCESTORS 31
CHAPTER 6: BOOMERANGS: MORE THAN JUST A PIECE OF WOOD 42
CHAPTER 7: ETHICS AND MORALITY IN ABORIGINAL LEGENDS 50
CHAPTER 8: DEATH, REBIRTH, AND THE AFTERLIFE 59
CHAPTER 9: NATURE AND ITS LINK TO ABORIGINAL MYTH 65
CHAPTER 10: SPIRITS OF THE OUTBACK 73
CHAPTER 11: ABORIGINAL WARRIORS WHO FOUGHT FOR THEIR LANDS 82
CONCLUSION 92
HERE'S ANOTHER BOOK BY ENTHRALLING HISTORY THAT YOU MIGHT LIKE 94
FREE LIMITED TIME BONUS 95
BIBLIOGRAPHY 96
IMAGE SOURCES 99

Introduction

Aboriginal mythology has been handed down through generations. These stories are far more than just entertainment; they are the stories of one of the world's oldest living cultures.

These narratives do more than narrate the dawn of time. They serve as lessons, moral compasses, and a means of connection to every aspect of the Aboriginal people's surroundings—from the tiniest grain of sand to the expansive heavens. Central to these tales is the Dreamtime, which represents the start of existence and whose spirits continue to shape the world.

Map of Aboriginal people's regions in Australia.[1]

Australia's landscape is as diverse as its stories, stretching from the red sands of the desert to the lush green of the rainforests to the deep blues of the ocean. This land has nurtured hundreds of Aboriginal nations, each with its own unique language, traditions, and stories.

With such a variety of cultures and communities, it is no wonder that the stories vary so much from one place to another. In one region, you might hear about the Rainbow Serpent, a powerful being that shapes the land and controls the water. Travel elsewhere, and the serpent's story changes.

These tales and stories are often filled with characters and symbols that might seem fantastical at first glance. They are filled with ancestral beings, talking animals, and forces of nature personified. However, they are more than just characters in a story. They represent deep connections to the land and to each other. Their tales talk about where to find water, how to read the stars, and the ways animals move with the seasons or even their breeding months.

The stories you will encounter are more than just historical artifacts. They are living lessons on sustainability, community, and the sacredness of the natural world. They challenge us to consider our impact on the earth and inspire us to forge deeper connections with the land.

A respectful reminder to Aboriginal and Torres Strait Islander readers: This book includes references to and images of people who have passed away.

Chapter 1: Dreamtime Creation Myths

It all began with nothing. It all started in the Dreamtime.

Before the clock began to tick and before the first calendar pages were turned, there existed a magical and mysterious period known as the Dreamtime. Dreamtime is like a mythological period of time in which life and the entire world came into being.

There isn't just one narrative that talks about how the earth and its inhabitants came to be; instead, there are many stories, reflecting the vast array of Aboriginal peoples and their deep connections to the land and its spirit. Some traditions tell of the earth's creation by gods of the Dreamtime, while others recount how specific animals, plants, and features of the landscape were brought into existence by different gods or ancestral spirits.

For several Aboriginal peoples of southeastern Australia, there was a very special celestial being known as Baiame. Baiame was a creator god, a powerful being who came down from the sky to shape the earth during the Dreamtime.

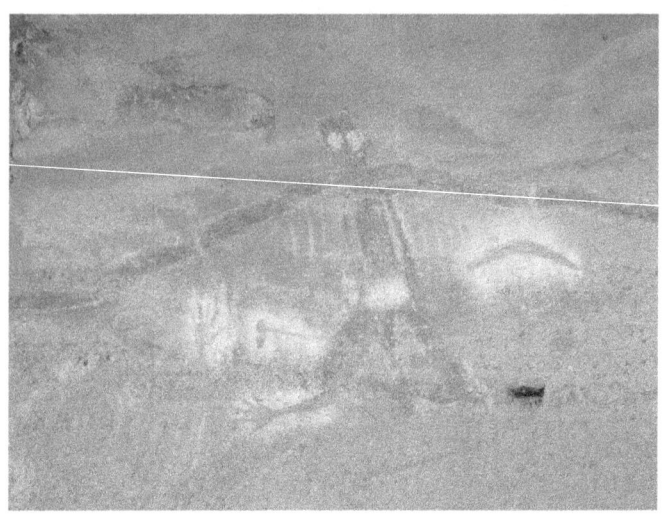

A painting by the Wonnarua depicting Baiame located near Milbrodale (to the south of Singleton, New South Wales).²

From his seat in the heavens, Baiame looked down upon the world, which was in complete darkness. What he saw was nothing else except a vast emptiness. There were no mountains standing tall, no rivers winding through the land, no trees swaying in the breeze, and no animals scurrying or soaring. The earth was silent and still.

Baiame decided it was finally time to create. He descended from the sky, touching the ground with the tips of his toes. Where his feet touched, the earth bloomed and came alive. Mountains rose up, reaching for the sky, and valleys emerged.

Next, the creator god sang, his melody weaving through the air, helping to give life to his surroundings. Rivers burst forth from the ground, dancing their way across the land. Then, trees sprouted up, reaching their branches high as if to catch the notes of Baiame's song. Flowers bloomed miraculously, filling the earth with a burst of vibrant colors.

The job was not yet done. Baiame knew the world would never be complete without creatures to roam, swim, and fly across it. So, with his divine abilities, he created a collection of animals and scattered them around the world. The kangaroo hopped across the plains, the emu strode through the grasslands, and the koala found its home among the branches of the gum trees (also known as eucalyptus trees). Fish filled the rivers, and birds flapped their wings in the skies. All kinds of creatures filled the land.

Baiame looked upon his creation with a smile.

"It is almost complete," he said.

The divine being moved on to his next creation. After gathering the dust of the earth, he carefully molded the first humans. He breathed life into them and taught them to live in harmony with the land. He showed them how to make shelters to protect themselves from nature and how to care for one another. Of course, Baiame also taught them the most important tool of survival: how to find food and water.

The first two humans gave birth to children, and their children gave birth to their own sons and daughters.

Baiame was generous. He gave much knowledge to the humans, ensuring that they could not only survive but also progress. However, he had one rule.

"You may eat these plants to sustain yourselves. But not the animals that I have created," Baiame said.

The grateful humans abided by his law. They lived in harmony with the earth and each other, just as the creator god had instructed them. That was the case until they were forced to face Mother Nature's wrath about a year later.

Mount Yengo, situated in the Wollombi Ranges near Awaba (Lake Macquarie), New South Wales, Australia. It stands solitary in the landscape. It is said that after Baiame completed the creation of the earth, he returned to the spirit world by leaping from this mountain, which he flattened in the process.[3]

The earth began to change, and the seasons turned unpredictable. Fierce storms swept across the land, causing the humans to remain in their shelters. Then came the extreme drought. Crops failed, and the forests that had once teemed with life now whispered of hunger and despair. The people, once nurtured by the abundance Baiame had gifted them, found themselves struggling to survive in a world that seemed to have turned against them.

In desperation and perhaps guided by necessity, one man decided to break the harmony Baiame had taught them to cherish. The man, who was accompanied by his wife, hunted and killed a kangaroo. Some of the animal's flesh was offered to one of their friends, who was visibly losing weight due to the lack of food and drink. However, much to their surprise, their friend refused the meat despite being sick from hunger. The man remembered Baiame's warning, and after continuously refusing the offer, he rose to his feet and walked away.

Confused, the husband and wife gave only a shrug before continuing to enjoy their meal. Once they were done, their friend's actions began to weigh on their minds. Had they said something to offend him? Or was there some hidden message in what he did that they were meant to decipher? The more they pondered, the more their curiosity grew. The couple decided to go and check on their friend, hoping they could persuade him to finally eat.

After packing some food with them, the two went on their way. They carefully followed his trail, which led them to a river. They saw their friend lying under a tall gum tree across the river. The husband and wife wanted to reach him, but the stream was too swift for them to wade or even swim across. They wondered how their friend even managed to cross the river.

Suddenly, the couple saw a black figure emerging from the branches of the tree right above their friend. They squinted their eyes to get a better look at the figure, and they were stricken by horror at what they saw. The creature appeared to be half-man, half-beast. Panicked, the husband and wife shouted to warn their friend, who was still sleeping under the tree. However, their friend was unable to hear them; he wouldn't have been able to hear them even if he were wide awake. The creature picked up the man, who was still not moving, and carried him into the branches, disappearing from sight.

From there on, a few more mysterious events took place. A burst of smoke shot out from the very same gum tree where their friend was resting. The couple kept on watching, their hearts pounding rapidly, as the tree began to move. It was as if the tree had come alive, lifting itself off the ground, roots snapping like twigs. The tree then soared across the river, flying south. As it glided by, the husband and wife spotted something even more chilling: two menacing, bright eyes peeking out from the shadows of the tree and two white cockatoos, flapping their wings wildly as if trying to catch up with the flying tree, which had possibly been their shelter all this time.

Before they knew it, the tree, the cockatoos, and those eerie glowing eyes had become just a tiny dot in the distance, far away to the south and high up in the sky. The husband and wife were made to realize that they had witnessed, for the first time, the event of death. The creature that they saw was Yowi, the spirit of death.

Just a few moments ago, he was seen alive. The next minute, he was dead, just like the kangaroo that had been killed for food by the husband and wife. All living things mourned upon learning of what had happened to the man.

This story, drawing particularly from the lore of the Kamilaroi (also spelled as Gamileroi or Kamilroi) tribe, narrates a profound moment when death is introduced to the world created by Baiame, the creator god. The tale is rich with symbolism and carries deeper meanings related to the cycles of life and death, the balance of existence, and the relationship between humans, nature, and the spiritual realm.

Another prominent Dreamtime story that tells the creation of the world comes from the Kamilaroi tribe. This narrative also begins with a description of how, in the beginning, there was only darkness as the world was asleep, waiting for a certain spark to ignite the dawn of creation. This spark came in the form of Yhi, a being of light and life. Her deep slumber was disturbed by the sound of a mysterious whistle. Some stories also suggest that Yhi was awakened by Baiame. The moment Yhi's eyes fluttered open, light cascaded upon the earth for the first time, piercing the veil of darkness and introducing warmth to the cold, barren land.

However, that was only the beginning of the story. Wherever Yhi wandered, the ground beneath her feet was said to have burst into life. The earth was covered in verdant green. Yet, Yhi yearned for more than just the stillness of the fauna; she envisioned a world filled with movement and dance.

To fulfill this quest, she delved deep into the earth, where she encountered evil spirits that tried to overwhelm her with their sinister songs. More than once, they tried singing her to death. However, Yhi's radiance was too powerful, and her warmth dispelled the shadows. The malevolent spirits were transformed into a multitude of insects, which Yhi brought forth into the world.

Her journey did not end there. The creator discovered ice caves hidden within a mountain that had long become a shelter for slumbering creatures. With her light, she awakened these beings. Fishes slipped into the streams, lizards scurried into the sunlight, and the air was filled with all sorts of birds.

Her quest was complete. Having breathed life into the earth, Yhi returned to her celestial realm. Before she left, she gave her creations the gift of seasons—a cycle of life, death, and rebirth—as well as a promise to place her creations among the stars when their time on Earth ended.

However, her departure brought darkness once more. The creatures, fearing Yhi's absence was permanent, mourned her loss. Thankfully, their sorrow was short-lived. For with the dawn came the first sunrise—a daily reminder of Yhi's presence and the promise of her return.

As time passed by, the animals began to grow restless. Yhi heeded their call. She descended from the heavens to hear their desires. First, she listened to the kangaroo who wished for the freedom to leap. Then, she listened to the wombat who yearned to burrow in the earth. The seal wanted to swim. The lizard told the creator about his wish to have legs to roam the land, and the bat told her of his dream of having wings to explore the skies. The platypus wished for a bit of everything. Yhi granted their wishes.

Yhi noticed that man was unlike any other creature she had fashioned. She also noticed the man's loneliness in the vast world. As he slept, Yhi focused all her energy on a single flower, imbuing it with her essence. The next morning, the man awoke to find the companionship of animals and a woman, who had been born from the flower.

Yhi had ensured that every creature had a place and a partner. With her task now done, Yhi ascended to the sky once more, her heart content.

Chapter 2: Songlines and Their Spiritual Significance

In the past, Aboriginal people did not rely on compasses or even stars to navigate the land. Instead, they relied on songlines that serve as invisible threads that link the physical world to the spiritual world. Each songline is a lyrical pathway, charting routes across the land and the sky through verses that tell stories of landmarks, waterholes, and sacred sites.

The origin of songlines is rooted deep in the Aboriginal creation stories known as the Dreamtime. Ancestral beings traversed the barren, formless land. As they moved, they sang the world into existence, their voices calling forth mountains, rivers, plants, and animals. These songs did not just shape the physical features of the landscape but also laid down the pathways that their descendants would follow.

Imagine for a moment that you were an Aboriginal traveler living thousands of years ago. To navigate the continent, you are equipped with not a physical map but songlines sung by the elders. These songs describe the landmarks you will see along your journey, from towering mountains to hidden springs. Each verse is a step, and each rhyme is a guide to the next landmark. By singing these songs, you can navigate vast distances, even through territories that you have never set foot in before.

It is crucial to follow these paths with respect and mindfulness. For Aboriginal people, the land is imbued with sacredness. A songline often dictates not just the path but also the direction in which it should be traveled. Deviating from this path or going in the wrong direction can be seen as disrespectful or even sacrilegious. A notable example is Uluru, the majestic sandstone monolith in the southern part of the Northern Territory, Central Australia.

Uluru is more than just a geological wonder. According to the Anangu, the traditional custodians of Uluru, this place is deeply embedded in the Dreamtime. The myths surrounding Uluru tell of ancestral beings who roamed the earth during creation. They shaped the landscape and created laws. Uluru is believed to be the physical evidence of their activities, making it a deeply sacred place where the earth's spiritual energy is palpable.

The ancestral stories associated with Uluru involve epic tales of battles, with features of the rock thought to be the marks left behind by these beings. For the Anangu, every crevice, cave, and natural formation on Uluru has a story. Ceremonies and rites are performed there to maintain the harmony between the spiritual and physical worlds.

Recognizing the sacredness of Uluru and in response to the longstanding wishes of the Anangu people, climbing on Uluru was officially banned in October 2019. For decades, the Anangu had requested visitors not to climb Uluru, as doing so was seen as a desecration of a sacred space. The act of climbing not only disrespected traditional laws and beliefs but also posed a physical risk to the climbers and caused environmental damage to this precious site. The ban on climbing Uluru represents a significant step toward recognizing and honoring the cultural rights and spiritual practices of Aboriginal Australians.

The sacred Mount Uluru.[4]

Songlines vary throughout Australia, reflecting the unique geography, flora, fauna, and cultural significance of each region.

- **The Yolngu People of Arnhem Land:** They recount the journey of Barnumbirr, a creator-being symbolized by the planet Venus. Originating from the island of Baralku in the east, Barnumbirr is celebrated for guiding the first humans to Australia. As she flew from east to west, Barnumbirr named and created the landscape's features. Her journey across the sky at dawn is still seen as a guide for the Yolngu people, reminding them of the eternal link between their ancestors and the land.

- **The Yarralin People of the Victoria River Valley:** They venerate Walujapi, the Dreaming Spirit of the black-headed python. Walujapi carved a snakelike track along a cliff face. The impression of her buttocks, which were left as she established camp, is a sacred site.

- **In the Sydney Region:** With valleys often ending abruptly in canyons or cliffs, the ridge lines become natural pathways. Songlines in this area predominantly follow these ridges, where the journey is easier and where sacred art, including the Sydney rock engravings, is found. This contrasts with other parts of Australia, where songlines might meander through valleys, drawn toward water sources and the sustenance they promise.

The Wirangu and the Seven Sisters Creation Story

For generations, the Wirangu people have been the heart and soul of the wild western coast of South Australia. They are the land's traditional custodians. The Wirangu people's heritage, passed down through countless generations, speaks of their deep relationship with this place, where the fierce ocean hits the rugged cliffs and reaches inland to the desert sands.

The Wirangu people's understanding of the world around them is deeply embedded in their language and cultural practices, which honor the land as a living entity. Every element of the natural world holds significance, from the smallest grain of sand to large boulders, as each carries stories from the Dreamtime.

The arrival of European settlers in the 1800s marked the beginning of a tumultuous period for the Wirangu. This era brought a wave of dispossession, cultural disruption, and a decline in population. The settlers, driven by a desire to claim and cultivate the land, often failed to recognize the sacredness of the earth and the intricate ties that bound the Wirangu to their ancestral territories.

One of the most harrowing episodes of this period was the events that unfolded around Elliston and Streaky Bay. In 1849, at least twenty-five Wirangu people, along with members of other Indigenous groups, were driven from the cliffs at Elliston to their deaths in the ocean below. For years, the areas around Elliston and Streaky Bay became taboo.

Yet, the spirit of the Wirangu proved resilient. In recent years, efforts have been made to acknowledge this painful chapter of Aboriginal history. To honor the lives lost, a memorial was erected at Elliston in 2017 after consulting with the Wirangu and other Aboriginal communities. Today, the monument serves as a place for reflection and healing. People often gather there to pay their respects.

Central to this journey of reconnection is the Wirangu people's songline creation story involving the Seven Sisters or Kungkarangkalpa. This tale begins in the Dreamtime when the world was young and the spirits roamed the earth, shaping the land and imbuing it with life.

The Seven Sisters are ethereal beings in the sky who descended to the earth one day, bringing with them radiance and beauty that were unknown to the land below. Their appearance was said to ignite an insatiable desire among the men who witnessed them. Completely enchanted and overwhelmed by their beauty, these men decided to pursue the sisters, hoping they could make them their lifelong companions. However, the sisters used their digging sticks to repel these advances.

However, the narrative takes a turn with the introduction of Wati Nyiru, also known as Yurlu, a sorcerer. Yurlu's desire to take one of the sisters as his wife was thwarted by his skin color. He was not of the correct skin group, a crucial aspect of the Aboriginal tradition that governs social and marital relations to maintain harmony and prevent close genetic intermingling. Despite this, Yurlu's infatuation spurred him to follow the sisters, hoping to overcome any barriers.

Yurlu's pursuit was marked by determination and the use of sorcery and shapeshifting. He would bend the will of the cosmos to his desires. Even though he managed to capture one of the sisters at Pangkapini, the sisters escaped time and time again. The eldest of the sisters was said to have taught her siblings to transform themselves into trees. This was done so they could hide from Yurlu and rest.

Eventually, the sisters made their way from the sands of Pirilyi to the waterhole at Puyatu, where they sought refuge in a cave. Yurlu refused to let a moment pass without having both of his eyes on the sisters. He watched them from a distance, his presence marked today by a stone mound believed to represent Yurlu's figure spying on the Seven Sisters.

Knowing that Yurlu had his eyes on them, the sisters planned their escape. Instead of exiting out of the only entrance to the cave, the sisters used their digging sticks to dig out a secret hole at the back of the cave. Once they were done, the sisters quickly escaped, hoping they could lose Yurlu.

In a desperate act, Yurlu employed his sorcery once again. He sent his phallus, in the form of a carpet snake, to chase the Seven Sisters. The snake was said to have slithered across the vast land, attempting to locate the women. The Seven Sisters noticed the snake, though. Mistaking the creature for food, one of the sisters took the snake. Little did they know, Yurlu had been trailing the snake all this while and was a step closer to capturing the Seven Sisters.

However, the Seven Sisters realized the danger they were in and tossed the snake into the horizon before fleeing. And so, the pursuit resumed. As the Seven Sisters fled from Yurlu across the varied landscapes of Australia, their journey left an impact on the earth. With every step and leap, they shaped the world beneath their feet, creating the world as we know it today.

As they moved, the Seven Sisters used their digging sticks, creating craters and valleys. The natural features formed by the sisters' journey were more than geographical landmarks; they were places imbued with meaning. Their path, which cut across the territories of the Martu, Anangu, Pitjantjatjara, Yankunytjatjara, and Ngaanyatjarra peoples, wove a network of songlines that stretched across the continent.

The Seven Sisters ascended to the heavens, seeking refuge among the stars, and transformed into the Pleiades constellation. Yurlu refused to give up. The sorcerer followed the sisters to the sky, continuing the pursuit for eternity. Even today, we can see the Pleiades constellation being chased by the constellation Orion.

A widefield view of the Pleiades.⁵

Interestingly, the significance of the Seven Sisters' journey is not confined to Aboriginal Australian culture alone. The Pleiades constellation holds an important place in numerous cultures around the world. The ancient Greeks saw them as the daughters of the Titan Atlas and the Oceanid nymph Pleione, and the Native Americans interpreted the constellation's appearance as a sign to begin the harvest.

A one-dollar silver coin issued in 2020 by the Royal Australian Mint that features the Seven Sisters.⁶

Yurlu never gave up his pursuit. His desire propelled him upward. He, too, became a constellation.

Yurlu became Orion, which is one of the most recognizable constellations in the night sky. In many cultures, Orion is depicted as a hunter perpetually following the cluster of stars known as the Pleiades. The positioning of Orion and the Pleiades serves as a cosmic reenactment of the Dreamtime story, with the gap between them symbolizing both the physical distance and the cultural laws that keep Yurlu from achieving his desire.

Chapter 3: The Lore of the Rainbow Serpent

Serpents slither through myths and legends of cultures around the world, often embodying chaos and destruction. In Egyptian mythology, Apophis (also known as Apep) was a formidable force of chaos. This enormous serpent dwelled in the darkness of the underworld and perpetually thwarted the sun god Ra's journey during the night. This age-old story symbolizes the eternal struggle between order and chaos.

Farther north, in the cold realms of Norse mythology, lives Jörmungandr. Known as the World Serpent, this creature was born of the trickster god Loki and the giantess Angrboda. Jörmungandr is described to be extremely enormous. It encircles Midgard (the realm of humans) until it can bite its own tail. This monstrous serpent is fated to release its grip only at Ragnarök (the end of the world). When this time comes, Jörmungandr will emerge from the sea to poison the sky and battle the thunder god Thor, which will lead to their mutual destruction. Jörmungandr symbolizes the inevitable end of all things.

The Rainbow Serpent of Aboriginal mythology diverges significantly from these narratives of destruction. It is far from being a monstrous entity. The Rainbow Serpent is actually revered as a powerful creator being, a life-giver whose presence and actions were integral to the birth of the landscape and life itself.

The Rainbow Serpent as the Creator of Beings

The Rainbow Serpent is known by many names across the continent, such as Ngalyod by the Kunwinjku people of Arnhem Land, Borlung by the Miali people of the Northern Territory, and Goorialla by the Lardil people of Mornington Island. The difference in names reflects the multifaceted role the Rainbow Serpent plays across Australia. For the Kunwinjku, Ngalyod represents the dual nature of the serpent as both a giver and taker of life. Borlung highlights the serpent's power over rain and storms. The spirit could bring life to the land but was also capable of causing floods. For the Lardil, Goorialla symbolizes the serpent's journey across the land, shaping the rivers, hills, and valleys that dotted the landscape.

According to the Wiradjuri people, the story of creation begins with Baiame, the sky father and creator god, who sent the Rainbow Serpent to the earth. This celestial being's arrival marked the beginning of the transformation of a world that was once empty and flat. After emerging from underground, the Rainbow Serpent began its journey across the continent. With every movement, the Rainbow Serpent's body carved out the contours of the earth, creating mountains, rivers, and gorges.

As the Rainbow Serpent traversed the barren lands, it encountered beings that had yet to realize their purpose. The Rainbow Serpent realized there was a great need for water to nurture the lifeless earth, and it called upon the frogs. The Rainbow Serpent coaxed the frogs into releasing the waters they hoarded. As the frogs laughed and danced, water burst forth, filling the rivers and gorges carved by the Rainbow Serpent.

A rock painting of the Rainbow Serpent.[7]

From these waters, life sprang forth. Trees stretched their limbs toward the sky, their leaves capturing the light and casting shadows on the ground below. Flowers bloomed in vibrant hues. Animals of all kinds emerged, from the smallest insect to the largest mammal. The land, once silent and still, now teemed with the sounds of life.

With its task completed, the Rainbow Serpent grew tired. It was said to have slithered away, claiming his hard-earned rest.

The Rainbow Serpent is also credited with the creation of humans. According to one story, after breathing life into the animals of Australia, the Rainbow Serpent taught them to live in harmony with each other. But some refused to obey the serpent's will; they caused trouble and argued with each other.

"I will gladly turn those who lived by my laws into humans," the serpent said. "Those who disobeyed will be punished. You will be turned to stone and never walk this earth ever again."

The Rainbow Serpent followed through on his threat. Those who had sown discord and refused to live in harmony were transformed into stone. Their forms became the mountains and hills that dot the landscape, becoming eternal reminders of the consequences of disregarding the laws of harmony. Those creatures who embraced the Rainbow Serpent's teachings were elevated to human form. Each was bestowed with a totem reflecting their animal, bird, or reptile origins—kangaroo, emu, carpet snake, and others—marking their tribes and connecting them to the land.

This division of totems among the tribes was not arbitrary. By decreeing that no individual should consume the animal of their totem, the Rainbow Serpent created a system of mutual respect and interdependence. This ensured that no species would be overhunted, preserving the balance of the ecosystem.

The Rainbow Serpent as the Protector of Water

In the Kuninjku language of Arnhem Land (located in the Northern Territory), the Rainbow Serpent is known as Ngalyod, a being linked to water sources such as creeks and rivers. This ancestral spirit is responsible for the lush vegetation that thrives near water, including water lilies, vines, and palms.

The Rainbow Serpent's dwelling, believed by some Aboriginal cultures to be within waterholes, has to be approached with care to avoid invoking its wrath. While not inherently a creature of destruction, the

Rainbow Serpent is capable of summoning storms, high winds, and rain. The Indigenous people engage in a specific ritual to announce their presence and intentions to the Rainbow Serpent. By singing out to the Rainbow Serpent, they signal their knowledge of the place and their respect for the traditions connected to it.

Did you know?

Maraiin ceremonies are deeply revered and sacred events that span several days. They feature an intricate blend of song and dance. During these ceremonies, song men (a title for respected men who are keepers of the sacred stories and songs) perform narratives of the ancestral beings' heroic deeds. They are accompanied by the rhythmic beats of a clapstick player and a didgeridoo. The song cycles dedicated to the Rainbow Serpent are of great importance. The ceremonies also celebrate the Water Goanna, which is believed to have created waterholes across western Arnhem Land before transforming into a goanna. In a captivating display, large wooden effigies of the Rainbow Serpent and the Water Goanna are carried by dancers to the ceremonial ground. Here, participants mimic the movements of these revered figures, paying homage to their roles in the natural world and cultural heritage.

The people also take a handful of earth and rub it on their bodies, a gesture that allows the Rainbow Serpent to "smell" them. It is a way of showing that they come in peace with no intention to harm or disrespect the Rainbow Serpent's home. After these rituals are observed, the people can approach the waterhole to drink.

Goorialla, the Rainbow Serpent Who Tricked the Rainbow Lorikeet Brothers

The story of Goorialla, the Rainbow Serpent, is an integral part of Aboriginal Australian mythology. It specifically originates from the Dreamtime stories of the Northern Territory. The story has been popularized through children's literature, notably by authors Dick Roughsey and Percy Trezise, who adapted this Aboriginal tale into a format accessible to younger audiences.

Goorialla's tale begins with his departure from the southern regions of Australia. He was driven by a desire to locate his kin. As he moved northward, he molded the once flat and featureless land into hills, valleys, and waterways.

Goorialla was welcomed enthusiastically by his people. The people engaged in song and dance, which Goorialla observed with keen interest. However, he soon noted discrepancies in their ceremonial practices. After asserting his authority, Goorialla corrected their dances and attire, instructing them in the proper ways of performing a ceremony. This intervention highlights Goorialla's role not just as a creator of the physical world but also as a custodian of cultural knowledge and practices.

However, the joyful reunion was soon overshadowed by a formidable storm. As the community braced for the tempest, everyone sought shelter in hastily constructed humpies (a type of simple temporary shelter commonly built by the Aboriginals). Among them were the Bil Bil brothers, two rainbow lorikeet (a species of small, colorful parrots native to Australia) who found themselves without refuge. In their desperation, they approached Goorialla, who deceitfully promised them shelter. Goorialla actually swallowed the brothers whole.

Fearful of the consequences once the community realized the brothers had disappeared, Goorialla fled. The clan traced Goorialla's path to a mountain. The Goanna (an Australian monitor lizard) brothers undertook a daring rescue. Scaling the mountain, they found Goorialla asleep. They managed to free the Bil Bil brothers from his belly. The brothers, now transformed into birds, escaped.

Goorialla awoke to the sounds coming from his empty stomach. In his rage, Goorialla threw bits of the mountain across the landscape. These bits turned into the hills and mountains we see today. Some of the people wanted to evade Goorialla's wrath, and they transformed into various forms of wildlife. By the time his anger diminished, only a small part of the original mountain—the one he had once rested on—remained. He then slithered down the small hill and made his way into the sea, where he was believed to be to this day. The legend concludes with a reminder of the responsibility humans have toward the natural world, a world that was once populated by beings who now exist in the form of animals, birds, and insects.

Another version of the story focuses on the aftermath of Goorialla's actions. After swallowing the brothers, Goorialla ascended to the sky, the only place he believed he could be safe. From his celestial vantage point,

Goorialla witnessed the profound sorrow of the people mourning the loss of the young men. Moved by their grief, he sought to atone for his actions.

Goorialla decided to transform his body into an arc of vibrant colors stretching across the sky. This transformation was his way of expressing remorse for taking the rainbow lorikeet brothers. In the moments following a rain shower, the Rainbow Serpent's colors can be seen in the sky. This appearance serves as Goorialla's apology.

Chapter 4: Aboriginal Constellations and Celestial Myths

The Aboriginal Australians have long held an important connection with the cosmos, telling stories as intricate as the constellations overhead.

For the Aboriginal people of Australia, the stars were not merely a spectacle of light in the dark sky; they were a map, a calendar, and a library of endless knowledge passed down through generations. Without the telescopes and gadgets that modern astronomers depend on, they had to understand the heavens above them. Doing so allowed them to predict when the seasons changed, when it was time to harvest, and when it was time to move.

They knew that when the emus in the sky run, it was the best time to hunt the creature and collect its eggs. When they caught a glimpse of the star Parna (Fomalhaut) in the morning, they knew that the annual autumn rains would arrive soon and that it was time for them to build large waterproof huts.

One Dreamtime story tells the origin of a certain constellation and a crater. This is the tale as recounted by Aunty Mavis Malbunka, the custodian of the Western Arrernte people of the Central Desert.

Long ago, in the Dreamtime, a group of women existed in the form of dazzling stars. With the Milky Way as their stage, they performed a corroboree, a sacred dance ceremony. The night sky became alive with their movements, as if there was a celestial ballet that celebrated creation. One of these women was a mother, and she brought her baby to this cosmic gathering. As she grew tired from the dance, the mother placed her child, cradled in a coolamon (a type of wooden basket or vessel), on the edge of the Milky Way. The mother then rejoined the other women.

The baby, perhaps stirred by the music of the cosmos or the gentle sway of the coolamon, slipped off the edge of the Milky Way and began tumbling toward the earth. The descent was silent, a falling star unnoticed against the backdrop of a billion others, until the baby and the coolamon struck the ground with great force.

This phenomenon formed a ring-shaped mountain range that is 5 kilometers wide and 150 meters high. This place, known to some as the Gosses Bluff Crater, is known by the Arrernte as Tnorala. To the Arrernte, this giant crater, formed over 140 million years ago by a cosmic event, hid the baby from the cosmos. Because of this, the baby's parents—the morning and evening stars—never reunited with their child. However, they never give up, and the search continues to this day.

Air view of Tnorala or the Gosses Bluff Crater.[8]

The Arrernte people hold this site in deep reverence, as it is a place where the veil between the earthly and the celestial realms is thin. Visitors are welcome to witness the site, but they have to be respectful.

The story can also be seen in the winter sky; visitors may have a chance to see the constellation known as Corona Australis right below the Milky Way. Its arc of stars represents the falling coolamon.

The Corona Australis as seen by the naked eye.⁹

The Markers of Seasonal Change: Pleiades, Baidam, and Arcturus

Also known affectionately as the Seven Sisters—though many more stars comprise this cluster—the Pleiades are a sight to behold. It is nestled within the constellation of Taurus. The Pleiades begin their ascent in the dawn sky just as winter starts to announce its arrival. The sight of Pleiades is a prelude to the colder months that lie ahead.

To the naked eye, the star cluster appears as a delicate mist of light. Through the lens of a telescope, the Pleiades reveal their true splendor— each star is a fiery beacon with blue-white hues.

This star cluster has served as a guide and a symbol for the Aboriginal Australians for millennia. The appearance of the Pleiades heralds the peak of the dingo breeding season. To the Aboriginal people, dingoes are companions in the cold winter nights, a source of warmth, and, during times of scarcity, a source of nourishment.

The Pleiades.[10]

However, the significance of the Pleiades extends beyond the dingoes. The bush tomatoes (kutjera), honey ants (tjala), and thorny devils (mingari) are all linked through interrelated traditions and songlines to this star cluster.

Another important constellation takes the form of a shark. It is known as Baidam among the Torres Strait Islanders (one of Australia's two distinct Indigenous cultural groups). Since sharks play a crucial role in maintaining healthy marine ecosystems—they are apex predators that help control the populations of other species—Baidam is considered to have been a symbol of life and sustenance.

Baidam's form is outlined by the seven bright stars that make up the Big Dipper, which is part of the larger constellation Ursa Major. As Baidam makes its grand entrance into the night sky, it signals a time of abundance and renewal, a period when the Torres Strait Islanders prepare the soil for planting crops of sugarcane, sweet potato, and banana. When the nose of this celestial shark touches the horizon right after sunset, it marks the start of the shark breeding season.

To the west, in the traditions of the Wergaia people of Victoria, another story unfolds. In the heart of a land parched by drought, where the sun scorched the earth until it cracked, there lived a people on the brink of despair. Food was just a memory, and the rivers and billabongs (a body of water in Australia often formed when a river changes course) that once teemed with life were now silent. In these dire times, a woman named Marpeankurric rose.

Marpeankurric knew that surrendering to despair was not what her ancestors would do. She set forth into the wilderness, her eyes looking for any sign of food. Days melted into nights under the relentless sun, and the land offered nothing. However, Marpeankurric's resolve was as bright as the stars in the sky above her.

Finally, fortune finally smiled upon Marpeankurric. Hidden beneath the cracked earth, sheltered from the prying eyes of the sun, lay a nest of wood ants, which her people referred to as bittur. Marpeankurric unearthed the nest to reveal thousands of ant larvae, which were more precious than pearls. Without hesitation, Marpeankurric tasted the larvae, finding them not only edible but also surprisingly flavorful.

Marpeankurric hurried back to her people, her heart overjoyed. Because of Marpeankurric's courage, her people were saved, and the ant larvae became an essential food source during the winter months.

However, Marpeankurric's legacy did not end with her earthly journey. In recognition of her valor and the lives she saved, she was honored after she passed away. Marpeankurric ascended to the heavens, her essence immortalized as the bright star Arcturus.

Arcturus, the brightest star in the constellation of Boötes.[11]

Arcturus is a giant star in the Northern Hemisphere, and it is brightest in the evening sky from late spring to summer. To see Arcturus, one needs to gaze toward the west shortly after sunset, where it shines as the brightest star in the constellation of Boötes, the Herdsman. Its appearance signifies that it is time to harvest ant larvae.

Other Constellations and Their Significance

Constellation	Description	Narrative/Significance
Yurree and Wanjel	Represented by the stars Castor and Pollux in Gemini. Yurree is the fan-tailed cuckoo, and Wanjel is the long-necked tortoise.	These stars symbolize two hunters in pursuit of the kangaroo, Purra. Their appearance in the sky marks the cuckoo's activity season and the tortoise's egg-laying time.
Purra	Symbolized by the star Capella, representing the Red Kangaroo.	Purra appears in the sky from August to February. It is followed by two hunters, Yurree and Wanjel.
Warepil	Centered around Sirius, Warepil is the male wedge-tailed eagle. This figure is significant across Victoria.	Known as Bunjil in Melbourne, Warepil represents leadership and creation.
Neilloan	Vega is the anchor star for Neilloan, which depicts the malleefowl.	The constellation is visible in autumn mornings and disappears in spring evenings. This aligns with the malleefowl's nesting and egg-laying season.

Brolgas	Illustrated by the Large and Small Magellanic Clouds (a pair of galaxies), these stars form the constellation of Kourtchin, showing a pair of dancing brolgas (a kind of bird).	Visible all year in Victoria's dark skies, this constellation celebrates the joyous dance of the brolgas.

The Story of the Evil Emu

At the dawn of creation, the great ancestor spirit Bunjil sculpted the world, giving birth to the majestic sandstone ranges of Gariwerd, also known as the Grampians. Transforming into Warepil the Eagle, Bunjil soared high, his eyes reflecting the beauty of his creations, from the whispering waterfalls to the towering gum trees.

Near the heart of Gariwerd, Bunjil found a place from where he could watch over the ranges. There, immortalized in Bunjil's Shelter, he stood with his faithful Wirringan, the dingoes who served as his eyes and ears. To bring order to this new world, Bunjil summoned the Brambram-bult brothers, children of Druk the Frog. Their task was to name the creatures, bestow languages, and lay down the laws that would govern everything.

As Bunjil ascended to the heavens, becoming a star that would forever watch over the land, a shadow loomed on the horizon. The emu Tchingal, a creature of darkness, roamed the mallee scrub. In its nest lay a colossal egg.

One day, Waa the Crow, driven by hunger, happened upon Tchingal's nest. The sight of the unguarded egg was too tempting. As Waa pecked at the shell, savoring the taste, Tchingal returned. The emu was enraged to see what was happening to its unborn baby. Waa quickly realized the gravity of the situation and took to the skies, fleeing toward the sanctuary of Gariwerd. Tchingal was hot on his trail, though.

As Waa approached the ranges, he spied a crack in the mountains. Darting into the crevice, he believed himself safe, but Tchingal struck the mountain with a force that shook the earth to its core. The mountain yielded, birthing Barigar, also known as Rose's Gap, and from its heart, a stream was born.

Tchingal pursued Waa through the newly formed gap. In a desperate bid for safety, Waa found another crevice, but again, Tchingal's might was unstoppable. Tchingal split the rock, creating Jananginj Njaui (Victoria Gap), where the Glenelg River escapes to the plains. As dusk embraced the land, Tchingal ended his pursuit, marking the place where the sun bids farewell. Jananginj Njaui means "the place where the sun will go."

The following morning, Waa sought refuge in Moora Moora swamp, a place sacred to him and where Tchingal's fury could not reach him. Yet, Tchingal's hunger for vengeance remained unquenched. It was then that Bunya, a man of the land, caught Tchingal's gaze. Bunya fled at the sight of the emu, abandoning his spears. Bunya climbed a tree, hoping for salvation among the branches. Tchingal waited below.

Word of Tchingal's evil reached the Bram-bram-bult brothers, who vowed to end the emu's reign of terror. Approaching under the guise of night, they found Tchingal. From the shadows, they launched their spears, striking Tchingal. Wounded, the emu fled toward the northern plains, its blood giving birth to the Wimmera River. Eventually, Tchingal died.

Bunya, still perched within the tree, hesitated to descend as fear clouded his judgment. In response to his cowardice, the elder brother transformed him into a possum, condemning him to a life among the treetops and seeking sustenance in the night.

The brothers then plucked Tchingal's feathers before splitting each of them down the center. They threw the split feathers, half to their right and the other half to their left. These two separate piles of emu feathers then transformed into the emus that we see today. Interestingly, the splitting of the feathers can still be seen on present-day emus; their feathers appear double with two separate halves.

Right before they moved on, the Bram-bram-bult brothers had to make sure no egg would ever spark such envy and strife again. They ordered the two new emus to divide their large egg into a few smaller ones.

In the heavens above, the story of Tchingal and the Bram-bram-bult brothers is etched among the stars. The Southern Cross, with Bunya at its head and the spears as its points, narrates the tale. Waa the Crow shines as Canopus.

The Southern Cross, also known as the Crux, as seen by the naked eye.[12]

Although Tchingal is seen as a terrifying adversary, it's important to recognize that the emu holds a place of reverence and respect among Aboriginal peoples across Australia. The Wiradjuri people, among others, see emus as creator spirits. These majestic birds play a crucial role in the Dreamtime stories that map the spiritual and earthly worlds.

The Emu in the Sky constellation, unlike the more defined constellations crafted by stars, is a dark constellation. It is traced not by the light of stars but by the dark spaces in the Milky Way, which creates the silhouette of an emu stretching across the night sky. This constellation is visible in the Southern Hemisphere's autumn and winter skies.

As the constellation rises in the sky, it signals the time for collecting emu eggs, a practice shared by many Aboriginal communities across Australia. Emu eggs are not only a valuable food source but also hold cultural and spiritual significance. One Dreamtime tale tells the story of how the egg became a symbol of light. It began when the emu named Dinewan argued with the dancing bird, Brolga. As the quarrel went on, Brolga became so angry that he snatched an egg from Dinewan's nest before launching it into the sky. The egg then landed on a heap of firewood and broke open. The yolk suddenly burst into flames, lighting up the entire world below. This act created the sun.

Chapter 5: Totemic Bonds: Animals and Ancestors

If you search what a totem is on the internet, it will most likely tell you that a totem is a natural object, animal, or phenomenon that serves as an emblem for a group of people. However, this explanation barely scratches the surface of totemic bonds among the Aboriginal Australians.

Totems are not arbitrary; they signify a person's or clan's connection to their ancestors, the land, and the Dreamtime. These connections are viewed as real and living, influencing daily life and social structures.

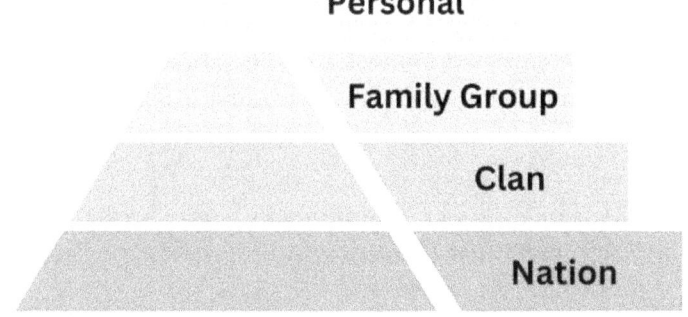

Totem structure in Aboriginal culture. (Created by author)

At the broadest level, the nation totem represents the collective spirit and identity of an Aboriginal nation. For example, the Wiradjuri Nation's totem is the gugaa, or the goanna. This creature embodies the qualities associated with the Wiradjuri people, such as resilience and strength. The nation totem links individuals to their wider community and the ancestral lands they inhabit.

Clan groups within these nations have their own totems, which act as identifiers and signify the unique characteristics or historical narratives of the clan. Strangers meeting for the first time can identify each other by their totems. Totems can signal who is likely to be friendly or not based on shared or complementary totemic affiliations and the intricate laws governing social interactions within and between different groups. This system has historically helped maintain peace and order and facilitated marriages and alliances of Aboriginal societies.

Another crucial aspect of this totemic identity is that it sort of determines who individuals can and cannot marry. In Aboriginal culture, people are not allowed to marry someone who shares the same totem as them. This is so that close relatives will not accidentally marry each other, preventing any health issues from appearing in future generations. This tradition also ensures diversity; people can create stronger bonds between different clans or family groups.

The personal totem is chosen by elders to reflect and honor the distinct qualities, strengths, and potential of a person. Unlike the inherited totems (the nation, clan, and family totems), the personal totem is assigned based on the individual's character, talents, life journey, or even weaknesses. This assignment is not bound by a specific timeline; it can occur at any stage of life. A child whose identity and inherent gifts are clear might receive their totem early on, allowing it to serve as a guide and protector through their formative years. For others, their personal totem might not be revealed until later in life. This flexibility ensures that the totem truly resonates with the individual's personal journey and growth.

The concept of moiety further deepens the totemic system's complexity. Moieties divide communities into two complementary halves, with each individual belonging to one moiety or the other. This division extends to totems.

For example, one moiety might have the gray kangaroo as a totem, while the other has the red kangaroo. Members of the gray kangaroo moiety are tasked with conserving and protecting the animal. The red kangaroo moiety might have permission to hunt and use the gray kangaroo but only within sustainable and sacred boundaries. This reciprocal arrangement ensures the survival of both species.

Of course, one of the cardinal rules within this system is that an individual is not allowed to harm or kill their own totem. This prohibition is rooted in the belief that the totemic animal or object is an ancestor, kin, or spiritual guardian. Harming it would be akin to harming one's own family or oneself.

Such responsibilities extend beyond mere protection or use. For example, the "emu people" are not only responsible for safeguarding emus but are also custodians of knowledge regarding their breeding cycles, habitats, and behaviors. This custodianship means that should an emu nest be raided or the birds' reproduction cycle be disturbed, the emu people are held accountable. They are expected to educate others, enforce protective measures, and rectify any harm to their totemic animal.

The totemic system acknowledges that while humans have needs that may involve using natural resources, they also have the duty to conserve, protect, and pass on a healthy and vibrant environment to future generations. Totems instill a sense of unity and interdependence that is central to Aboriginal cultures.

Examples of Totemic Animals

Totemic Animal	Region	Aboriginal Group(s)
Kangaroo	Various, widespread across Australia	Wiradjuri (New South Wales), Pitjantjatjara (Central Desert)
Emu	Various, widespread across Australia	Wiradjuri (New South Wales), Wotjobaluk (Victoria)
Crocodile	Northern Australia (Northern Territory, Queensland)	Yolngu (Arnhem Land), Gagudju (Kakadu National Park)

Wedge-tailed Eagle	Victoria	Kulin nation, Wurundjeri
Turtle	Northern coastal areas (Queensland, Torres Strait)	Torres Strait Islanders, Coastal Queensland groups
Dolphin	Coastal regions, especially in Western Australia	Noongar (Southwestern Australia)
Brolga	Northern and northeastern Australia	Guugu Yimithirr (North Queensland)

Dreamtime Stories of the Kangaroo

The kangaroo is one of the most iconic creatures in Australia and holds immense cultural significance for Aboriginal Australians. The Arrernte people of Central Australia, for instance, revere the red kangaroo, which they refer to as kere aherre. Similarly, the Palawa people from Flinders Island, Tasmania, have the kangaroo as their totem. Despite the geographical distance and environmental differences from the mainland, the kangaroo is still an important symbol for the Palawa people.

Red kangaroos at Sturt National Park.[18]

Interestingly, the name "kangaroo" has its origins in the language of the Guugu Yimithirr people of far north Queensland. The word *gangurru* refers to a specific type of kangaroo and was first recorded by James Cook and his crew during their exploration of the region.

The animal's significance is not only due to the kangaroo's prominence in the Australian landscape but also because of its vital role in Indigenous cultures. For Aboriginal Australians, kangaroos have always been integral to their way of life, serving as a crucial source of food and playing a part in rituals, Dreamtime stories, and oral traditions.

The Dreamtime story of Bohra the kangaroo is a great example of the relationship between Aboriginal people and the kangaroo. There once was a time when an impenetrable darkness shrouded the world each night, making it impossible for the bright moon and stars to shine. During this time, a creature named Bohra roamed the land on all fours. Although he was adept at navigating the dim world, especially when he fed at night, he longed to see the world bathed in the gentle glow of the moon and stars. Instead of sitting by and hoping something would change, Bohra chose to take action.

As a wirinun, or a magician of great power, Bohra rolled the darkness away, as if it was a rug covering the night sky. This allowed the moon and stars to light up the heavens, enabling him and other creatures to see clearly during the night.

Later, Bohra found himself drawn to the sight of fire and the melody of distant singing. His curiosity led him to a sacred gathering—a corroboree of tribespeople moving rhythmically around a fire. Moved by an irresistible urge, Bohra stepped into the light, tentatively rising onto his hind legs in an attempt to join the dance.

The tribespeople were taken aback by the sight, but at the same time, they were enthralled by Bohra's presence. He continued to dance awkwardly, trying to mimic their movements. However, as a consequence of intruding on the sacred corroboree uninvited, the tribal wirinun declared that Bohra must be punished. Since he had shown the tribe a new dance, the punishment of death was ruled out. Instead, Bohra and his descendants would be bound to move by jumping on their hind legs, using their forefeet as hands and their tails for balance. This curse also granted Bohra a place within the tribe, signifying the kangaroo's enduring bond with Aboriginal people.

Bohra's canine teeth were knocked out as part of his initiation into the tribe. The men of the tribe fashioned false tails, adorning themselves to mimic their new kin. The kangaroo dance, born from that night, became an integral part of their sacred rituals.

Another Dreamtime tale tells of how the kangaroo got its tail. There once lived two friends: Mirram the kangaroo and Warreen the wombat. In those days, both Mirram and Warreen were men, and they walked the land in harmony.

Warreen had a knack for craftsmanship, and he constructed a lovely humpy or gunyah for himself. This small, temporary shelter, woven from soft bark and lined with leaves, offered him a cozy refuge. Mirram, on the other hand, found comfort in the soft grass beneath him, which served as his mattress, and the star-studded sky above, which he considered his quilt. The thought of a shelter never crossed his mind.

That was until the skies opened up one day, unleashing a heavy downpour that Mirram had never seen before. Mirram was soaked to the bone and, shivering, sought refuge in Warreen's gunyah. Warreen refused to let Mirram enter. Left out in the cold, Mirram's frustration brewed into a storm fiercer than the one raging around him.

Mirram conceived a dark plan. He dragged an enormous rock to the entrance of Warreen's shelter. Mirram smashed the rock upon Warreen's unsuspecting head. The impact startled Warreen and flattened his head. However, by some miracle, his life was spared.

"Oh, you wicked Mirram. How could you hurt your dearest friend?" Warreen asked.

"A friend? You are mean and selfish, Warreen!" Mirram angrily responded.

A wombat in Narawntapu National Park, Tasmania.[14]

Warreen's thoughts turned to vengeance. He bided his time until an opportunity presented itself. One day, Mirram was chasing a possum. Warreen lifted a spear and stealthily approached Mirram. With a swift thrust, he pierced Mirram's back, embedding the spear so deeply that it became a part of him, transforming into a long, spear-like tail.

From that day forward, Mirram thumped the ground with his tail with every leap, a constant reminder of Warreen's revenge. He never again sought shelter. Warreen bore the mark of the rock's blow, and his descendants were forever distinguished by their flat heads, serving as a lesson for selfishness and the cost of revenge.

Wayamba the Turtle

The Arakwal people of Byron Bay, nestled in a picturesque coastal region, have long been guardians of the land and sea that define their home. Among the many totems revered by the Arakwal people is the turtle, or Binguing as they call it. Because of the Binguing, the Arakwal people know how to live in harmony with the marine environment, ensuring its protection for future generations. Even to this day, surfers and swimmers can often catch a glimpse of turtles swimming to the surface of the bay for air.

Byron Bay.[15]

"The turtle is a free spirit and can glide gracefully through the ocean for over a hundred years. Many people can see the joy in the spirit of a turtle because it lives as though it doesn't have a worry in the world."

-Luke Mallie, an artist of both Aboriginal and Torres Strait Island descent[1]

The Dreamtime tells the story of the first turtle. The story of Wayamba begins with Oola the lizard, who was out gathering yams on the Mirrieh flat with her three children. There was no danger in sight, and the mother and children took their time. However, their foraging was soon interrupted by the rustling of something large in the bushes. Oola squinted her eyes, trying to get a better look at what lurked in there. Suddenly, Wayamba burst forth, startling Oola and her three children.

Wayamba had no intention to harm them. He actually expressed his desire to take Oola as his wife. He even offered to bring her children to his camp. Oola was intimidated by Wayamba's spear and boondi (a type of hardwood club), so she reluctantly agreed to follow him to his camp.

However, upon their arrival, Wayamba's tribe expressed their discontent. They were furious that Wayamba had brought Oola and her children without seeking the approval of her tribe. They warned Wayamba of the inevitable conflict with Oola's tribe, as they would surely come to reclaim her.

"We shall not help you if they come," Wayamba's chief told him. "Now, you must go to the plains and do your own fighting."

As predicted, Oola's tribe soon arrived, their bodies covered in war paint and their weapons at the ready. Wayamba He armed himself with two large shields, one covering his front and the other slung against his back. He then took up his weapons. As he stepped onto the plains, the air was pierced by the sound of sharp spears and boomerangs launched by Oola's tribe. Wayamba drew his limbs inside the shields and ducked his head, miraculously surviving the onslaught.

---

[1] *Dreamtime Stories: The Turtle.* (2020, August 13). Yarn Marketplace.
https://www.yarn.com.au/blogs/yarn-in-the-community/dreamtime-stories-the-turtle
Dreamtime Story: The Seven Sisters. (2020, December 8). Yarn Marketplace.

The spears fell to the ground, but the attackers had no plans to give up. They closed in, forcing Wayamba to retreat toward a creek. Cornered and with no ground left to give, Wayamba discarded his front shield and leaped into the creek. Oola's tribe waited, their spears poised to strike should Wayamba resurface. However, their wait was in vain. Wayamba was never seen again.

Instead, in the waterhole where Wayamba had vanished, they encountered a peculiar creature they had never seen before. This being had a fixed plate on its back like a shield and could draw in its head and limbs when threatened. This marked the birth of the first turtle.

A hawksbill sea turtle, a critically endangered species.[16]

The Crow, an Animal of Tricks and Cunning

In another story of the Aboriginal people, particularly within the Kulin nation of central Victoria, the crow holds a place of great importance. Known in their tongue as Waa or Waang, the crow is regarded as one of their two moieties or ancestral spirits, with the other being the eagle-hawk Bunjil.

An Australian raven.[17]

One such legend told orally by the Wurundjeri people of the Kulin nation talks about the origin of fire, a gift that forever changed the lives of all beings. The secret of fire was guarded by the seven Karatgurk sisters who called the banks of the Yarra River (the location of urban Melbourne) their home. These women carried live coals on the ends of their digging sticks, which they used to ignite flames for cooking murnong yams, a staple in their diet.

One day, the crow stumbled upon a cooked yam lying on the ground. Upon tasting it, he was struck by the realization that cooked food was far superior to the raw fare he was accustomed to. This ignited a desire within him to cook his own food. He approached the Karatgurk sisters and asked them to share their fire. However, they refused; they were protective of the power they wielded.

Not one to be easily deterred, the crow devised a clever plan to obtain fire. He first caught several snakes before concealing them within an ant mound. Then, he invited the women over and told them he had just tasted ant larvae. He claimed they were exceptionally delicious, even more so than the cooked yam. Believing the cunning crow, the women decided to try the larvae. As they began to dig into the mound, they disturbed the snakes concealed in it. Angry, the snakes attacked the women, who let out loud shrieks. They began hitting the snakes with their digging sticks as hard as they could. In the ensuing chaos, the live coals were dislodged from their digging sticks. The crow swiftly collected the coals, stowing them away in a kangaroo skin bag.

When the Karatgurk sisters realized they had been tricked, they pursued the crow, who eluded capture by taking to the skies. From his perch high atop a tree, the crow watched his pursuers' efforts.

The commotion attracted Bunjil the eagle-hawk. He was intrigued by the crow's discovery of fire and requested some coals to cook a possum. Instead of handing one to the eagle-hawk, the crow offered to cook the possum. Word of the crow's possession of fire spread, leading others to demand he share this precious knowledge. In a moment of panic, the crow flung live coals to the crowd, and the fire-tailed finch, Kurok-goru, caught some. The finch tucked them behind his back, which is the reason why firefinches have red tails to this day. Bunjil's shaman helpers, Djurt-djurt the nankeen kestrel and Thara the quail hawk, also helped gather the rest of the coals.

A wedge-tailed eagle, a species that Bunjil is often depicted as.[18]

However, the scattered coals led to a bushfire, scorching the crow's feathers black. The fire threatened to engulf the land until Bunjil intervened. The Karatgurk sisters were swept into the heavens, turning into the Pleiades. Their glowing fire sticks shine down as stars and act as a celestial reminder of how fire came to people.

Chapter 6: Boomerangs: More Than Just a Piece of Wood

When speaking of Australia, some may immediately think of the boomerang, a piece of exquisitely crafted wood that flies back to the thrower. Known worldwide and often brought home by tourists as souvenirs, it is often seen as a cultural novelty. However, boomerangs actually hold a far deeper significance that goes beyond what meets the eye.

The Aborigines never thought of the boomerang as only a simple tool. Every inch of it contains a story. Its unique, circular flights, for instance, are thought to mirror the cycle of life, death, and rebirth; this is a central concept to Aboriginal spirituality where all things are interconnected.

Boomerangs come in various shapes and designs, and they are crafted with a specific purpose and cultural meanings. The most popular one is the returning boomerang. Known for its ability to fly in a curved path and return to the thrower, this type of boomerang is designed specifically for precision and control. Typically lighter, this type of boomerang often has a distinctive twist in its wings. This specific design allows them to catch the air and complete a full loop.

There are non-returning boomerangs. Designed for straightforward power, this type of boomerang flies in a direct line rather than returning back to the thrower. In contrast to the returning boomerang, this particular boomerang is usually larger and weighs significantly more.

With its symmetrical shape, a non-returning boomerang can maintain a straight, forceful path.

The cross boomerang serves a whole different function. With four equal arms extending from a central point, cross boomerangs are usually used for ceremonial purposes such as dances, storytelling, and rituals rather than hunting. They are often made from wood or metal and sport a hole in the center.

Since boomerangs hold a deeper significance to the Aboriginal Australians, it is not surprising when people put extra care into crafting one. The process starts with selecting the right wood. This is perhaps the most critical step. The choice of wood used can affect the boomerang's shape, weight, and, of course, durability. Mulga wood is known to be rather dense and strong, making it the perfect wood for boomerangs used for hunting. In contrast, she-oak is lighter and easier to carve out intricate designs. Boomerangs made from this wood are more suited for ceremonial purposes.

Regardless of the wood choice, it is also important to ensure that the wood is dry and free of knots and cracks. To ensure that the wood is suitable for shaping, the makers prefer to harvest wood straight from the branches or roots, which naturally have slight bends. However, there are some who prefer to use driftwood or fallen logs.

After choosing the right wood, the shaping process begins. To strip the wood down to a rough outline, the makers use an array of tools such as stone axes, knives, or controlled fire. The shape itself varies on the intended use. If someone is crafting a boomerang for hunting, the maker would shape it to be longer and straighter, making precision and impact the main attributes of the boomerang. Those intended for ceremonial use, however, are often fashioned with more unique curves or additional bends, making them appear more distinctive than the ones used for hunting.

Once the boomerangs are shaped, it is then time for them to be smoothed and polished. Makers utilize sandpaper, emery, or even animal skins to remove the rough edges and reduce imperfections. The ultimate goal is to refine the boomerang's surface so that it can slice through the air smoothly. It is only after achieving the right level of smoothness that the makers move on to the next step: decoration. This is where intricate carvings and paintings of animals, plants, and landscapes or tribe symbols are made to embellish the look of the boomerangs.

Of course, these decorations are not only for design; each of these cultural expressions carries a unique meaning. Boomerangs with an image of a kangaroo, for example, are thought to symbolize agility and resilience, while a snake embodies wisdom and transformation. As for the coloring process, the makers always make sure to use colors that are derived from natural sources, such as ochre, charcoal, clay, or plant juices. These colors are applied with either brushes, sticks, or fingers. Once the coloring process is done, the boomerang is covered in a protective layer of resin, wax, or oil so that it can withstand both Mother Nature and the passage of time.

Last but not least, the boomerang must be tuned. Its angles, balance, and aerodynamics are put to the test, ensuring that it can fly in the way it should. If needed, makers will bend or twist the wood, shave down certain parts of the boomerang, or add subtle weights to achieve the desired flight pattern. This is a process of trial and error; the makers will test and refine the boomerang until it meets their standards.

The Origins of Boomerang According to Dreamtime Stories

This Dreamtime story begins with the Rainbow Serpent resting on a hill. Under the sunlight, its scales glinted so shimmery that it caught the attention of a group of hunters. Enthralled by the beauty of the serpent's multicolored scales and consumed by greed, the hunters felt the desire to take the scales for themselves.

"There is only one way to do this," one of the greedy hunters said. "We have to kill the Rainbow Serpent."

Eager to get their hands on the beautiful scales, the hunters made their move. Slowly, they readied their spears and crouched closer to the resting serpent. With a fixed aim, they hurled their spears at the magnificent creature. However, their spears were no match for the mighty Rainbow Serpent, as its scales were extremely tough, perhaps imbued with magic and divine powers. The spears bounced off its scales, and surprisingly, they flew back toward the hunters. Seeing this, the greedy hunters immediately fled in terror; they realized they had underestimated the mighty power of the Rainbow Serpent.

This, however, is not the end of the story. Angered, the Rainbow Serpent eventually decided to teach the greedy hunters a lesson. The serpent uncurled its great body, plucked one of its own glinting scales, and hurled it after the hunters. This magical scale flew through the air in a wide curve and struck one of the hunters in the back. With fear completely overtaking them, the hunters fled for good. Knowing that the lesson had been delivered, the serpent was able to enjoy its peace once again.

As the great serpent was about to return to its rest, it saw one remaining hunter nearby. Unlike the others, this hunter had been the only one who had refrained from attacking the Rainbow Serpent earlier. So, the Rainbow Serpent rewarded him. The great spirit offered the wise hunter one of its shimmering scales and gave detailed instructions on how he could use it. This scale became the very first boomerang, serving as a tool of sustenance and survival for the Aboriginal people for countless generations.

The Binbinga people of northern Australia have told their own story that explains the origin of the boomerang. It also involves a giant serpent, which they refer to as Bobbi-Bobbi; its difference from the Rainbow Serpent is that Bobbi-Bobbi lived in the heavens, watching over the earth below. Bobbi-Bobbi was thought to be a gentle and benevolent spirit who never failed to help humans thrive.

The serpent, gazing down from the skies, noticed the humans' struggle. Despite having shelter and enough water, they were struggling to find enough food. So, Bobbi-Bobbi, always known for his compassion, decided to lend a hand. Using his magical powers, the giant serpent created flying foxes—a species of large bats native to Australia—so that the people could hunt them for meat and nourishment.

This did not solve the problem, as the bats soon flew too high for the humans to catch. Determined to see humans prosper, Bobbi-Bobbi came up with another creation. The giant serpent shaped one of his own ribs into the world's first-ever boomerang. He then handed down his new creation to the humans and taught them to throw it at the flying foxes. For this, the humans were grateful; they no longer had to battle with hunger every day.

However, humans could never escape their own greed. Despite being grateful for the gift, some wanted more. Two men, in particular, became curious and wished to see the heavens where Bobbi-Bobbi dwelled. They hatched a plan, and when others asked them about their intentions, the two pretended they wanted to thank the giant serpent in person. The two men threw the boomerang into the sky, slicing through the clouds and creating a hole in the celestial realm. This action startled Bobbi-Bobbi to the point he failed to catch the boomerang in time. It fell back to the earth, striking the two men who had thrown it. They were killed, marking the first time death ever confronted humans.

As for Bobbi-Bobbi, the giant serpent was terribly saddened by their reckless act. He retreated further into the heavens, never again interfering in human affairs.

The Eagle and the Crocodile: The Creators of the Boomerang

Another story that explains the origin of the boomerang centers around the Eagle. Held in high regard in many Dreamtime stories, especially for its strength and keen intelligence, the Eagle was also thought to be the ruler of the skies, watching over the lives of the creatures that dwelled below. One day, the Eagle spotted a group of kangaroos grazing peacefully. Hungry, the Eagle decided to capture one of them for a hearty meal.

The kangaroos, ever alert, quickly evaded capture the moment they saw the Eagle swooping down from the sky. Although frustrated, the Eagle was not one to give up; it attempted to capture one of the kangaroos again, only for the kangaroo to successfully dodge its sharp talons. At this point, the Eagle knew it had to be creative, as its usual hunting tactics were not working. After a moment of thinking, the Eagle flew to a nearby tree, where it snapped off a branch. With patience and precision, the Eagle shaped and molded the wood until it turned into a curved stick—a boomerang.

With this new tool, the Eagle returned to the skies and looked for the kangaroos. Once it spotted them, the Eagle threw the curved stick at them. The boomerang spun through the air in a wide arc. Finally, one of the kangaroos fell victim to this tool, stunning it long enough for the Eagle to swoop down and claim its long-awaited meal. Satisfied with its creation, the Eagle soon felt the need to share this new knowledge. It gathered other birds and taught them how to craft and use the boomerang.

While this story revolves around a hungry Eagle, there is another tale that speaks of the boomerang's origin. Almost similar to the tale of the Eagle, the Crocodile's story begins with the animal feeling a tinge of hunger as it rested in a river. Noticing a school of fish swimming near the surface, the Crocodile made a move; it snapped its powerful jaws, hoping it could catch at least one. However, these fish were too fast, and they darted away before the Crocodile's teeth could close around them.

The Crocodile tried again, yet he was met with only frustration. The fish were too slippery and swift. The Crocodile went away and swam to the riverbank. Upon stumbling upon a strong root growing nearby, the Crocodile began to think of an idea. After digging the root out, the Crocodile let natural instinct guide its creation. He eventually shaped the root into a curved blade using only his sharp teeth and claws.

The Crocodile quickly swam back toward the location where the fish were swimming. It hurled the curved blade at the water, and the boomerang spun in a slicing motion, cutting through one of the fish with ease. The Crocodile was impressed by his new creation, and he chose to share it with the other reptiles so that they could catch their prey more effectively.

Wurruna, the Young Hunter Who Ended Drought

There was a time when the earth was nothing but dry and barren. A skilled young hunter named Wurruna planned to save his people. Not only were rivers and ponds a thing of the past, but the once-abundant land now lay parched beneath the merciless sun, leaving his tribe starving. Wurruna knew it was only a matter of time before his people would succumb to the worst fate of all. Armed with his spear and club and accompanied by his two loyal dogs, the young hunter embarked on a journey to restore hope back to his land.

For a long time, he traveled across the vast plains and rugged hills, where he encountered an array of strange and wonderful creatures. He saw the prickly echidna scurrying across the dust, the elegant emu standing proud, and the kangaroo using its powerful hind legs to leap through the air.

Apart from animals, Wurruna also encountered an old man during his journey. The elder was said to have sensed the weariness in Wurruna's eyes, and he offered the hunter a gift: a magic stone that could produce water wherever it was thrown. Wurruna was overjoyed with the gift. He expressed his gratitude to the old man before placing the stone safely in his pack and continuing his journey.

Days later, the young hunter's perseverance finally paid off when he stumbled upon a lake brimming with fish. Wurruna set up his camp by the lake. Making use of his hunting skills, he cast his spear into the water, successfully catching several fish for a meal. He cooked them over a small fire and savored them. Suddenly, a creature appeared, flying above the lake in lazy circles. Wurruna concluded that it was none other than a brolga (a species of bird native to southeastern Australia and New Guinea). Captivated by the bird's beauty, Wurruna planned to catch the brolga and turn it into his pet.

The young hunter aimed his spear, and after a deep breath, he hurled it toward the brolga. However, Wurruna had underestimated the bird, as it easily dodged it. The brolga then let out a playful call, as if trying to mock Wurruna for missing. Not one to back down, Wurruna reached for his club and threw it at the mocking brolga. Again, the hunter missed. Interestingly, the club did not fall to the ground. Instead, it spun in a loop and made its way back into Wurruna's hand. Amazed by this new weapon, Wurruna named this creation the boomerang after the whirling sound it made as it spun through the air.

His excitement for this new weapon did not divert his attention away from the brolga. He threw his boomerang in the direction of the bird again and again but failed to bring the brolga down each time. The bird flew higher in the sky and taunted the young hunter even more. Wurruna chased after the bird and threw his boomerang again and again. But while doing so, he accidentally left a trail of water across the land. It turned out that his magic stone had slipped from his bag onto the boomerang. Each time he threw the boomerang, a small stream of water poured from the stone. This created rivers, lakes, and ponds across the landscape, transforming the barren earth into a planet full of life.

The cat-and-mouse chase went on between Wurruna and the brolga. The young hunter eventually managed to corner the bird at the edge of a steep cliff, where he threw the boomerang one last time. The brolga caught the boomerang mid-air with its beak and flew off into the sky. Wurruna could do nothing except watch the bird fly away with his new invention—and the magic stone with it. The young hunter was heartbroken. He fell to his knees, feeling as though he had lost everything.

The brolga, on the other hand, spotted a group of people who appeared to be celebrating something. The bird landed and found out that these people were from Wurruna's tribe; they had been following the trail of water that Wurruna had unknowingly left behind. When they found the newly formed waterhole nearby, the people gathered around to rejoice at the bounty that had returned to their land. Perhaps affected by their joy, the brolga decided to join in the celebration, dropping the boomerang and dancing around with the humans. The tribe welcomed the bird with open arms.

The boomerang, which had been left on the ground, was eventually found by Wurruna's loyal dogs. Recognizing that it was their master's previous invention, the dogs picked it up with their mouths. The magic stone was nowhere to be found, though. The dogs hurried back to the cliff where Wurruna remained in despair. The sight of his dogs carrying his boomerang filled the young hunter's heart with both gratitude and relief. He hugged his companions, thanking them for their loyalty.

As he stood and looked down the cliff, getting ready to move on with his journey, Wurruna noticed his tribe dancing and celebrating by the waterhole. He was surprised at first, but joy immediately took over as he realized that his journey had not been in vain after all. Although he had lost his magic stone and failed to capture the brolga, Wurruna had successfully brought back life to the land. Not only that, the young hunter had also created a tool that would benefit his people for generations to come. Perhaps embracing the wisdom of the journey, Wurruna chose to forgive the brolga for its mocking.

Upon joining his tribe in their celebration, Wurruna took the chance to show his people the boomerang, teaching them how to use the tool. The boomerang became a cherished part of their lives, and Wurruna was hailed as a hero.

Chapter 7: Ethics and Morality in Aboriginal Legends

Throughout the history of human civilization, myths have served as a foundational pillar. From the ancient Greeks to the Egyptians and the Norse, each culture has harnessed the power of myths to convey important lessons.

In Greek mythology, tales of Icarus, who flew too close to the sun, and Prometheus, who stole fire for humanity resulting in Zeus's wrath, underscore the dangers of overreaching one's ambition and the value of restraint. Egyptian myths emphasized the balance of Ma'at, or order, over Isfet, chaos.

Aboriginal myths and legends also imparted wisdom and ethical guidelines. Through these stories, knowledge, cultural values, and laws are transmitted from one generation to the next, ensuring the survival of Aboriginal heritage and wisdom.

Tiddalik the Frog

Back when the earth was very young, there lived a creature named Tiddalik the frog. Tiddalik was not an ordinary frog. He was small, mischievous, and greedy. One day, the glow of the sun woke Tiddalik from his short nap.

Tiddalik awoke with a thirst unlike any he had felt before. Driven by this insatiable desire, Tiddalik began to drink. He drank from the billabongs, their waters cool and refreshing. He drank from the rivers, where the fish darted in silver flashes beneath the surface. He drank from the streams, their babbling voices quieted by his endless thirst.

As Tiddalik drank, he grew bigger and bigger. However, the world around him began to change too. The billabongs shrank, their muddy beds exposed to the scorching sun. The rivers slowed, their currents weakened, and the streams whispered no more. The land became parched, and the trees drooped. The animals gathered in the dwindling shade, confused. As Tiddalik drank, the water in the world began to disappear.

Soon, the creatures of the land came together to voice their concerns. They knew that if Tiddalik's thirst was not quenched, the world would be devoid of water. A wise wombat came up with a plan. They would make Tiddalik laugh; if he laughed, the water he had consumed would surely be released, returning to the world.

The animals decided to host a corroboree, where they began their attempts to entertain Tiddalik. The first to come forth was the kangaroo. He danced, his legs kicking up dust in a comical display. Yet, Tiddalik did not even crack a smile. Next, it was the lizard's turn. He waddled on his two legs, making his stomach stick out. The other animals laughed at his silly act, but Tiddalik remained unfazed.

"Surely a little joke or a funny story would make him laugh," said the kookaburra. However, the kookaburra also failed to entertain Tiddalik.

A kookaburra, a bird native to Australia, known for its laughing call.[19]

Hope was beginning to disappear until the arrival of Nabanum the eel. Nabanum danced in front of Tiddalik. His body contorted into outlandish shapes. He danced and danced, his speed increasing until he accidentally entangled himself into a knot. There was a moment of silence. Tiddalik could not contain himself. A chuckle bubbled up from his huge belly. He then let out a burst of laughter that shook the leaves from the trees and ruffled the feathers of the birds.

As he laughed, the waters he had consumed burst forth in a great deluge. This filled the rivers, streams, and billabong. The animals sighed in relief.

Tiddalik returned to his initial form. He realized that it was not nice to be greedy and that sharing will always make the world a better place. Tiddalik reminded himself to take only what he needs when he needs it.

The story of Tiddalik teaches that personal needs and desires must be balanced with the well-being of others, a lesson of moderation and communal responsibility that is as relevant today as it was in the Dreamtime.

Though versions of this story are found in many Aboriginal cultures, it is often attributed to the Gunaikurnai people of South Gippsland, Victoria. The story of Tiddalik is thought to have been inspired by the behavior of the water-holding frog (*Ranoidea platycephala*), an amphibian native to central Australia. These frogs have developed an extraordinary adaptation to their arid environment. They burrow underground during dry periods, emerging with the rains to absorb significant amounts of water. This unique behavior allows them to breed, feed, and, most importantly, avoid drying out during times of drought. In times of scarcity, Indigenous Australians would gently squeeze these frogs to obtain water.

The *Ranoidea platycephala*, commonly known as the water-holding frog.[20]

However, the original tale, as recounted by some Aboriginal groups, ends with a rather somber reflection on the consequences of Tiddalik's actions. In this older version, the flood resulting from Tiddalik's laughter does not just replenish the world; it also brings about an environmental catastrophe. The flood causes widespread drowning, with many animals losing their lives and others finding themselves stranded on newly formed islands. Borun the pelican came to the aid of those stranded, ferrying them to safety.

The story of Tiddalik, in all its variations, teaches us about the importance of living in harmony with nature, the dangers of greed, and the responsibility we have to protect and preserve the world for future generations.

Another Aboriginal story that centers around the theme of greed involves the intriguing tale of two brothers-in-law, Gandji and Wurrpan. One warm day, Gandji, accompanied by his children, ventured to the water to spearfish for stingrays. With skill honed by years and patience, they speared several stingrays. The catch of the day was bountiful, and with spirits high, they set about preparing their feast.

They cleaned and filleted the fish. They gathered firewood to cook their catch, the air heavy with the scent of the sea mingled with the smell of smoke. The division of their spoils cast a shadow on their success. They wrapped the stingrays in bark, creating two portions—one filled with the succulent pieces and the other with the tougher parts.

Upon returning to their camp, Gandji presented Wurrpan's family with the lesser portion, keeping the more delectable share for himself and his children. Wurrpan and his family immediately noted the poor texture and taste. When Wurrpan learned of the unfair division, he confronted Gandji, arguing that fairness dictated the better pieces to be shared equally between their families.

Gandji was taken aback by the complaint and retorted, "If you desired the sweeter flesh, you should have taken to the waters yourself instead of awaiting our return." What started as a discussion soon escalated into an argument, with the two hurling insults at each other.

Neither side was willing to yield. In a fit of rage, Gandji grabbed a fistful of hot coals and a rock that he used for grinding nuts. He hurled them at Wurrpan, striking him squarely in the chest. Fearing that Wurrpan might retaliate, Gandji began to jump frantically, his leaps growing unnaturally high until he found himself soaring above the ground. As he ascended, his form began to morph. He grew feathers, and his body elongated into the shape of a bird—the jabiru—although he had no beak.

Wurrpan went to fetch his spear. Finding it too cumbersome, he shortened it before launching it skyward. His aim was precise. The spear pierced Gandji from the back of his head and through his face, making the protruding spear look like a beak. Gandji lost his balance, and he plummeted to the earth.

Wurrpan, with his children in tow, fled. As they ran, their bodies stretched into the slender, elegant forms of emus. Their feathers took on the gray hue of the ash from the coals, and a lump marked the spot where the smooth stone had struck Wurrpan. The unique shape of emu eggs mirrors the shape of the stone thrown by Gandji.

Lungkata the Blue-Tongued Lizard Who Lied

A blotched blue-tongued lizard, found in Tasmania, Australia.[21]

While the stories of Tiddalik and the skirmishes between Gandji and Wurrpan serve as moral lessons about greed and the consequences of selfishness, another tale from the heart of Australia emphasizes the importance of honesty.

Lungkata, a blue-tongued lizard man, traveled from the far north. He was drawn to Uluru because of its tales of beauty and community. He found a cozy cave that offered shelter and a splendid view of the sprawling landscape below.

One day, under the blazing sun, Panpanpalala, the crested bellbird man, was out hunting. With a well-aimed throw, he speared an emu. However, the emu, whose wings were too weak to fly, bolted toward

Uluru. The story sometimes whispers of Panpanpalala having a brother, making them a pair rather than a lone hunter. However, according to Jacob Puntaru, an Anagu elder, the most important thing about these stories is not the details but rather the lessons they teach.

Lungkata was also out searching for food. While he was on the hunt, his eyes fell upon the emu. It was wounded yet still breathing. He could see a spear lodged firmly in its side—a clear sign that it was already claimed by another hunter. Despite this, Lungkata decided to take the emu for himself, killing it with his stone ax. He then lit a fire and started to prepare his meal. However, not long after that, Lungkata heard the footsteps of an approaching stranger. It was Panpanpalala, who had been tracking his emu.

"Did you, by any chance, come across a wounded emu?" Panpanpalala asked.

Lungkata had managed to hide his stolen meal before Panpanpalala got close. He tried hard to conceal his panic.

"No, I haven't seen any emu," he answered.

Panpanpalala breathed a sigh of disappointment and left Lungkata alone. He had been tracking the emu for hours, yet there was no sight of it. But Panpanpalala eventually sniffed out Lungkata's deceit. He noticed the emu's tracks near where Lungkata had been camping.

Realizing the imminent return of Panpanpalala, Lungkata hastily gathered what he could of the emu meat and fled to the west. However, his escape was hasty, and he dropped a trail of pieces of the emu, including its thigh, which is still visible today at Kalaya Tjunta, just north of the Ikari cave near Mutitjulu Waterhole.

The path Lungkata left was glaringly obvious. It wasn't long before Panpanpalala caught up to him. Lungkata scrambled up Uluru, hoping he could escape from Panpanpalala and live another day. However, fate had another ending in store for the blue-tongued lizard. Under the watchful eyes of Uluru, Panpanpalala built a bonfire beneath Lungkata as the lizard struggled upward toward his cave.

The fire grew, eventually reaching Lungkata. Choked by smoke and licked by flames, Lungkata's desperate escape turned into a downfall. He tumbled down the face of Uluru, his body leaving a trail of scorched marks on the sacred rock. As he rolled, the heat stripped flesh from his body. Lungkata grew smaller, his form shrinking until all that was left of him was a single stone.

The Grim Tale of the Moonman

Before there was a moon to light the night sky, the Moonman walked the earth. He lived a simple life with his two wives and two sons. His wives were foragers, venturing into the bush to gather yams, berries, and plums, which sustained their family through the seasons.

As time passed, the two sons grew into teenagers. One day, filled with a burgeoning sense of responsibility and perhaps a dash of youthful arrogance, they approached their father with a declaration. They intended to go hunting. They wanted to provide for their family just as their father had always done. Moonman's heart swelled with pride at their words. He saw in them the reflection of his teachings and the promise of their growth into men of honor and skill.

And so, with their father's approval, the two sons set out to a big billabong. There, they showcased the skills their father had imparted to them, catching a variety of fish. A few hours later, their stomachs started grumbling, signaling that it was time for a hearty meal. They decided to cook a portion of their catch. Before long, a huge pile of fish sizzled over the fire, filling the air with tantalizing aromas.

Caught in the moment and seduced by their own greed, they feasted on the fish. With their hunger now satisfied, the two teenagers returned to their father bearing only the bony remnants of their selfish indulgence.

Moonman was delighted upon seeing his sons. However, his delight immediately dimmed when he discovered their haul was nothing but inedible bones. Stung by their father's disappointment yet unrepentant, the sons vowed to right their wrong. They promised a bounty of fish upon their next return. Yet, history repeated itself at the billabong. The lure of immediate satisfaction proved too strong, and once again, they indulged in the moment, leaving only bones to carry back to their father.

Moonman was outraged. He devised a devilish plan. First, he crafted a huge fishing trap out of kurrajong bark fiber. Once done, he handed it to his son.

"Let us use this trap when we go fishing another day," Moonman said to his sons.

The day eventually came. Moonman accompanied them to the billabong. He waited for the right moment, and as his sons lost themselves in the act of fishing, Moonman struck. Moonman used a big stick to beat his sons to death. He then left their bodies concealed within the very trap he had created and cast it into the billabong.

The next day, Moonman's wives returned from their foraging. They noticed the absence of their sons, so they immediately went to ask their husband. Unsurprisingly, Moonman chose to lie; he told his wives that their sons had gone fishing and that was the last time he had seen them. Upon learning this, the wives went to the billabong. There, they were confused by the water's crimson stain. They decided to pull the trap ashore and were struck by terror at what they found.

They cried for hours. Eventually, their grief morphed into anger. They carried the remains of their sons home. When the sky turned to night, the women set fire to their hut. Moonman was inside, deep asleep. He woke up seconds later, feeling as if he had been placed inside a blazing furnace.

Moonman screamed and made a desperate attempt to save himself. His escape led him to the top of a pandanus tree, where he declared his immortality.

"Remember this," Moonman shouted to his wives. "You'll disappear forever when you die. But I will come back immortal every month!"

In the heart of the Northern Territory is another tale of the moon's creation. This story centers around Japara, a man known far and wide for his exceptional skills as a hunter. Yet, this tale is really about hunting; rather, it is a story of love, loss, and redemption.

On a day like any other, while Japara was out providing for his family, a man named Parukapoli visited his home. Unlike Japara, whose prowess lay in tracking and spearing, Parukapoli's gift was in the art of storytelling. With a voice that could weave magic into words, Parukapoli told tales so captivating that Japara's wife became utterly entranced. She would become so absorbed in the stories that she would lose all sense of time and her duties. She did not even notice her baby son crawling away.

The baby's venture led him to a nearby stream, and he toppled into the water. Hearing the splash, Japara's wife rushed to save their son, but fate had already claimed the child.

When Japara returned and learned of the tragedy, his world crumbled. A fierce anger arose, and he blamed his wife for their loss. In a blind rage, he took up his hunting weapons and killed her. This act of violence was the spark that ignited a fierce confrontation with Parukapoli. The two fought each other, eventually resulting in Parukapoli's demise.

Left alone with his wounds and engulfed in a sea of grief, Japara faced the scorn of his tribe. They surrounded him, their voices raised not just in anger but also in disappointment. His actions had broken the sacred bonds of family and community.

"How could you kill your wife? She did not intend for any of this to happen!" they cried.

As the weight of his deeds settled upon his shoulders, Japara's heart began to open to the truth of his people's words. He returned to the location where he had left the bodies of his loved ones. Much to his sadness, the bodies were now gone; the spirits had taken them to a better place, a realm beyond his reach. Japara pleaded with the spirits, acknowledging his cruelty and expressing his yearning to be reunited with his family.

The spirits were moved by his remorse and granted him a path to the sky world, though not without conditions. As a penance for his actions, Japara was to wander the heavens, searching for his loved ones among the stars.

The moon that lights our night sky is said to be Japara's campfire, its glow a symbol of his eternal quest. The scars that mark the moon's surface remind us of Japara's earthly battles. Some say the moon waxes and wanes because Japara is forever changing camps. Others believe he has found them, and together, they explore the vast, mysterious expanse of the sky world.

This tale, like the moon's cyclical dance, speaks of the transformative power of love, the depths of despair, and the possibility of forgiveness. It reminds us that actions borne of anger can lead to irreversible consequences, but even in the darkest night, there is hope for redemption and reunion under the watchful eyes of our ancestors in the stars.

Chapter 8: Death, Rebirth, and the Afterlife

Back in the Dreamtime, a time when the world was young and the concept of death was unknown, the creatures of the earth lived in a state of perpetual existence. They never aged, and they never faded. Every morning brought the promise of infinity. However, this timeless tranquility was shattered one fine morning when a young cockatoo lost his grip while swinging high up in a tree. He fell, striking his head with such force that he lay still. The forest had never known such stillness.

The animals, bewildered by this unexpected turn of events, quickly gathered around. They attempted to wake the cockatoo from his peculiar slumber to no avail. The commotion soon drove the wise old wombat to see what could be done. He solemnly informed the others that their friend had broken his neck. The animals believed that this was the doing of the spirits. They had never witnessed their friends getting even the tiniest wound before, let alone death. The animals convened a meeting beneath a grand old gum tree to ponder this new dilemma.

During their discussion, the spirits lifted the little cockatoo into the sky, leaving the animals below to gaze in wonder as their friend ascended into the heavens.

"Worry not," the wise wombat said. "The spirits are doing no harm. They are merely transforming our friend into something new."

This notion sparked a mix of curiosity and hope among the animals. They asked each other who was brave enough to see if the wombat was speaking the truth. However, since winter had already blown its first cold breath, no one was eager to journey into the sky to witness the transformation—except for the caterpillars. The caterpillars ascended into the sky, hoping they could bear witness to the fate of their dear friend.

Days passed, and the animals, with the wise wombat leading the search, scoured the land for any sign of the caterpillars. They could find nothing. Then, on the first day of spring, the air was suddenly filled with a kaleidoscope of color. A parade of butterflies danced into view. The animals understood that the caterpillars had been reborn, transformed by the spirits into creatures of beauty and grace, just as their friend, the cockatoo, had been given a new form in the sky.

This transformation, the emergence of the butterfly from the cocoon, became a symbol of hope. This story tells us that change is an integral part of existence and a necessary part of life.

In Aboriginal culture, the journey through death and beyond is as deeply rooted in the community and the land as the journey through life. For the Aboriginal people, grieving is not merely an individual process. It is something that the whole community goes through together. They mourn not only to express sadness but also to embrace and celebrate the life and legacy of the person who has passed. This collective way of grieving undoubtedly helps to ease the pain.

Did you know?

It is considered deeply inappropriate for individuals outside of the Worrorra, Ngarinyin, and Wunumbal tribes to paint or depict the Wandjina. These sacred spirits hold immense significance within these communities, and their portrayal is reserved exclusively for those in those tribes. Recognizing the importance of protecting this cultural heritage, the image of the Wandjina was trademarked in 2015 in an effort to prevent its misappropriation. Despite these measures, unauthorized use of the image of the Wandjina continues, highlighting the ongoing challenges in safeguarding Indigenous cultural expressions.

While at a glance, the Aboriginal response to death bears resemblances to European traditions—most notably in the ceremonial acknowledgment of death and the observance of mourning—such comparisons barely scratch the surface. While ceremonies and mourning are universal across cultures, Aboriginal spirituality infuses these practices with a profound connection to the land. For example, loved ones are often buried on ancestral land, and smoking ceremonies are sometimes performed to cleanse and guide the spirit back to the land. Death, as much as life, emphasizes the inseparable bond between the individual and the land. The deceased is seen not as departing from this connection but as entering into a new phase of existence. However, they will be forever entwined with the country of their birth.

Aboriginal beliefs hold that when a person dies, aspects of their spirit, along with their bones, return to the land where they were born. Thus, when someone passes away, the land feels the loss so deeply that trees may die or bear scars.

The transition from the physical world to the afterlife is a journey of the spirit back to the essence of creation or, rather, the womb of all time (Dreamtime). Life is a cycle with no true end. The concept of an afterlife in Aboriginal culture is different from Western notions of heaven and hell; it is not a place of reward or punishment but rather a return to the Land of the Dead, a realm that coexists with the living world.

The belief in the indestructibility of the human spirit is central to Aboriginal spirituality. Upon death, the spirit does not cease to exist; it transitions into the everywhen—a realm where time is non-linear and the spirit becomes one with the elements of nature.

Smoking Ceremonies

Smoking ceremonies hold a significant place in Aboriginal culture, especially in the mourning process. These ceremonies are performed at the location where the person passed away and within homes. They serve as a purification ritual and a means to guide the deceased's spirit peacefully to the afterlife. During these ceremonies, it's not uncommon for relatives to express their sorrow through physical manifestations of grief, such as cutting their hair or adorning their faces with white pigment.

Among the Western Arrernte people, it is believed that the soul travels to a distant island, integrating into the Dreamtime where ancestral spirits reside and continue to influence the world. In a similar vein, the Wandjina, revered figures in the Dreamtime stories of the Kimberley region, play a unique role in the transition to the afterlife. According to lore, upon choosing the place they would die, the Wandjina painted their images on cave walls. They then entered nearby waterholes, marking their passage from the physical world to the spiritual realm.

Other Central Australian Aboriginal groups envision the Land of the Dead as a celestial realm, a place among the stars where the spirits dwell. These diverse beliefs shape the funerary customs and ceremonies practiced by Aboriginal communities. Everyone wants to ensure the spirit's safe passage to the Land of the Dead.

Aboriginal cultures place great emphasis on the performance of specific rites and ceremonies, both in life and after death. These rites are seen as crucial for the spirit's transition, and it is believed that it is only through the completion of these rituals that the spirit can successfully navigate its way to the afterlife. The relatives of the deceased play a vital role in this process, carrying out postmortem ceremonies with great care and respect to honor the departed and aid their spirit on its journey. If people ignore this, then the spirit will not be able to move on, and it will resort to disturbing its living families.

Sorry Cuts

"Sorry cuts" are another form of expression of grief within some Aboriginal cultures. In the wake of a loss, individuals may make small cuts on their bodies, allowing the blood to flow as a physical release of their inner pain. This practice is deeply personal and is often surrounded by cultural taboos, including restrictions on discussing these acts of mourning with grieving family members.

Ceremonies and mourning periods are elaborate and can last for days, weeks, or even months. It is considered culturally inappropriate for a non-Aboriginal person to inform the next of kin of a person's passing, as this task is reserved for those within the cultural kinship system. This way, it ensures that the news is delivered with sensitivity and respect for traditional protocols.

The Aboriginal communities practice a concept called "sorry business," which encompasses the various practices associated with mourning and remembrance. This period of sorrow is not only a time for grieving but also a time for the community to heal, bringing together families to share in the loss, remember the deceased, and reaffirm the bonds that tie them to each other and to the land. During "sorry business," communities engage in storytelling, singing, and dancing, all of which serve to honor the deceased and facilitate their journey to the afterlife.

In many Aboriginal communities, burial rites are intricate. However, despite the variations, a common thread is the deep respect and care for the deceased, ensuring their safe passage to the afterlife and maintaining the harmony between the living, the land, and the spiritual world. Here are a few examples:

Burial Method	Description	Regions / Groups Known to Practice
Earth Burials	The body is placed in a grave dug into the ground, with variations in orientation and depth. Personal items may accompany the deceased.	Widespread across many Aboriginal cultures in Australia.
Platform Burials	Bodies are placed on raised platforms and left exposed to the elements. Bones may be collected, painted, and then buried or stored after decomposition.	Practiced in some communities, particularly in Arnhem Land (Northern Territory).
Tree Burials	The body is placed in the hollow of a tree, allowing for natural decomposition in a protected environment.	Known among certain groups, such as those in parts of Queensland.
Rock Shelter Burials	Bodies or bones are placed in rock shelters or caves, which protect the remains. These sites can be marked or decorated.	Common in regions with suitable geographical features, like the Kimberley (Western Australia).

Water Burials	The body is set adrift on a canoe or placed directly into water.	Less commonly documented but practiced by some coastal and islander communities.
Secondary Burials	After initial decomposition, remains are collected for a second burial. It often involves rituals like painting bones with ochre and wrapping them for reburial.	Various Aboriginal cultures across Australia, with practices varying significantly between groups.

The Aboriginal practices of honoring those who have passed tell a story of life's unending rhythms. These traditions remind us that death is not simply an end but is also a passage—a bridge to something beyond our immediate grasp. This perspective shifts the weight of grief into a celebration of the natural cycle that connects all beings. It paints a picture of a world where the essence of those who have left us still lingers in the land they cherished, in the gentle rustling of trees, the soft murmur of streams, and the subtle whispers carried by the wind.

Chapter 9: Nature and Its Link to Aboriginal Myth

The Great Barrier Reef is a marvel of the natural world. It stretches over 2,300 kilometers (1,429 miles) along the northeastern coast of Australia. While many admire the beauty of the reef, for the Aboriginal people, particularly the Yidinji of the Gimoy (Cairns) region, it is a source of sustenance and a sacred site imbued with stories and spirits that trace back to the Dreamtime.

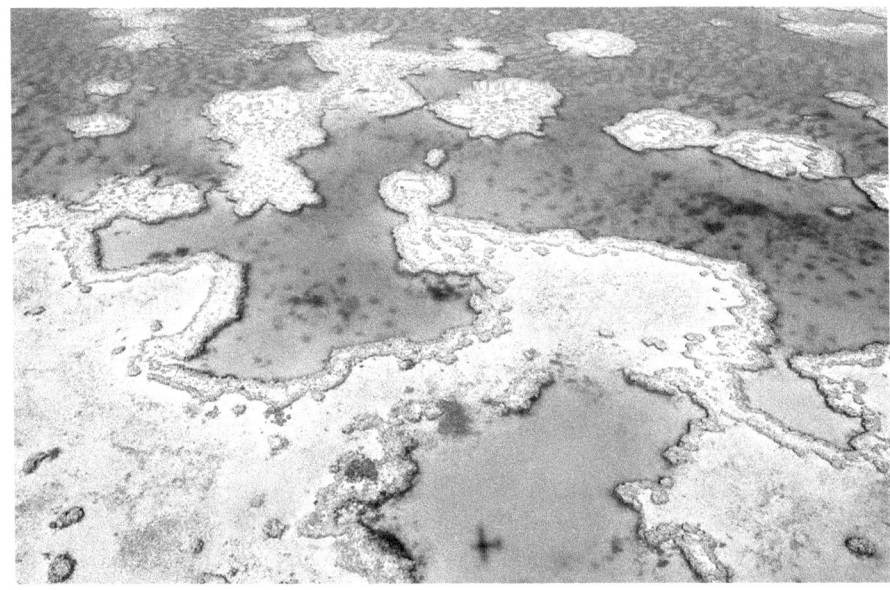

The Great Barrier Reef.[22]

One tale involving the Great Barrier Reef speaks of a time before the reef as we know it even existed. The story involves two brothers—others suggest a hunter and his two wives—whose actions brought them the wrath of their creator.

According to this tale, it all began with a creator named Bhiral placing a guardian fish in the sea where the Great Barrier Reef would soon form. This fish held such importance that it held the balance of the ecosystems in its fins. This particular fish was meant to keep harmony among the offshore islands. Bhiral, in his wisdom, had forbidden the spearing of this sacred creature; to harm it would be to unravel the very threads of life itself.

Yet, the brothers chose to defy the words of the mighty creator. They cast their spears into the water, striking the fish that was meant to remain unharmed. Their actions eventually reached Bhiral.

In his anger, Bhiral summoned the fire of the earth, hurling lava into the deep ocean. The sea boiled and rose. The brothers watched, their hearts sinking as the world around them changed. Where there was once only water, the cooling lava formed a new structure, a barrier that would stand as a reminder of their transgression. The Great Barrier Reef was born from their defiance.

These days, the Great Barrier Reef faces challenges that its ancient guardians could never have imagined. Marine scientist and coral specialist Charlie Veron—also known affectionately as the "Godfather of Coral"—has expressed profound sadness at the changes the reef has undergone. It has suffered from the impacts of climate change, pollution, and human activity. The corals, stressed by rising temperatures, have bleached, losing their colors and the life that once thrived among them.

The stories of the Yidinji and the teachings of elders and scientists highlight the urgent need to protect this precious ecosystem. In doing so, we honor not only the natural world but also the cultural heritage and wisdom that have been passed down through the generations.

Gulaga, the Mother Mountain

When Captain James Cook, the British explorer known for his voyages across the Pacific Ocean, first laid eyes on a majestic mountain along the southeastern coast of Australia, he named it Mount Dromedary due to its resemblance to a camel's hump. Little did he know, this particular mountain held a significance far beyond what he could have comprehended. To the Yuin people of southern New South

Wales, this mountain, known as Gulaga, was and remains a sacred site.

Gulaga Mountain from Bermagui on the south coast of New South Wales. [28]

Did you know?

In the face of recurrent bushfires and drought, nearly one hundred Yuin nation individuals gathered at the foothills of Mount Gulaga in early December 2019. Coming from as far as Sydney and Victoria, they convened for a healing corroboree, a nationwide dance aimed at healing the country's spirit and land. Djiringanj elder Warren Ngarrae Foster highlighted the event's timeliness, noting, "Minga Gulaga had been crying. She has called her children back to come together at her feet to heal the spirit and country."

Gulaga is not just a mere mountain; she is Mother Mountain, a powerful symbol of motherhood, nurturing, and protection. To the Yuin, Gulaga represents the sacred birthplace—the spiritual origin of life and culture of the Yuin people. It is a crucial site for women's ceremonies, storytelling, and childbirth. Indigenous artist Cheryl Davison captures the essence of Gulaga, stating, "She's always been here. Gulaga is the Mother Mountain. Pregnant, she lies on her side, her head to the south, her feet to the north, facing the sea ... She was here when the stars and the moon and everything else was created ... she's always been here."[31]

---

[i] https://www.nma.gov.au/exhibitions/endeavour-voyage/gulaga-mount-dromedary.

The Dreamtime story of Gulaga and her two sons, Baranguba and Najanuga, speaks to the themes of adventure, protection, and the maternal bond. One day, as they were collecting bush tucker (also known as bush food, referring to any food native to Australia), Baranguba expressed his desire to go fishing. Gulaga advised against it, saying he was too young and that it was dangerous to venture alone. Despite her warnings, Baranguba's longing for independence and the call of the sea were too strong to resist.

In one version of the story, Baranguba sneaks away, crafts himself a canoe, and heads to the sea, only to be met by a formidable wave that washes him away. He is forced to lie in the ocean, transforming into an island that remains a part of the landscape to this day. Another telling of the tale sees Gulaga eventually relenting to her son's wishes, allowing him to venture into the ocean but not too far from her watchful gaze. Baranguba sets out, lying down in the ocean and turning into an island under the protective eye of his mother.

Witnessing his brother's departure, Najanuga also yearns for a space of his own. Yet, Gulaga asks him to stay close to her feet. Najanuga becomes a symbol of the child who stays by the mother, representing those who remain close to their roots and the protective embrace of the family. Today, the rock outcrop known as Najanuga or the Little Dromedary can be seen just to the east of Gulaga.

The Dreamtime Story of the Barramundi, Australia's Most Iconic Fish

Nestled in the heart of the East Kimberley region lies the Argyle Diamond Mine. This site is renowned worldwide for its deposits of pink and red diamonds. This mine transformed the landscape and brought the Western world's gaze to this remote part of Australia.

Long before the land was excavated for its precious stones, it was the setting for a Dreamtime story that explains the origin of the diamonds found there today. This tale tells of Daiwul, the giant barramundi.

To the Aboriginal people, the barramundi embodies the connection between the physical and spiritual worlds. This fish is an important part of Aboriginal people's dietary habits and is often represented in Aboriginal artworks that narrate the ancient stories and laws passed down through the generations. One such contemporary artwork by June Peters, an artist from Warmun, vividly brings to life the Barramundi Dreaming.

As the tale goes, Daiwul was no ordinary fish. She was colossal, and her skin shimmered with the promise of the Dreamtime. As she swam through the waters of Bow River, Daiwul caught the attention of three women. Perhaps enthralled by the barramundi, they decided to set out to catch Daiwul. In an attempt to get their hands on the shimmering fish, the women pushed down a wall of spinifex (a species of grass native to Australia) down the creek, hoping it could trap Daiwul. However, Daiwul leaped over the trap set by the women.

A barramundi.[24]

As Daiwul jumped over the hill behind Bow River, her underbelly scraped against the hill, causing a crack to form. The scales from her underbelly scattered across the countryside and became diamonds. Known as "rain stones" by the local Aboriginal people, they were believed to possess the power to summon rain when struck together and thrown into waterways.

At Gawinyin, or Cattle Creek Rockhole, the three women turned to stone, standing as eternal guardians at the water's edge. Visitors to the area can still witness these stone figures.

While Daiwul's tale narrates the origin of diamonds in the Kimberley region, another captivating dreamtime legend tells about the creation of the barramundi itself. This story tells of two young lovers bound by a love so immense that it defied the laws set by their tribe.

The lovers, whose union was forbidden under tribal law, chose to follow the call of their hearts. In a bold act of defiance, they fled, seeking refuge in the land and hoping to escape the consequences of their forbidden love. However, their tribe would not let them go so easily. As the lovers made their desperate escape, they were pursued relentlessly until, at last, they found themselves standing at the edge of the ocean with nowhere left to run.

It was in this moment of ultimate desperation that the young man turned to face his pursuers, throwing his spear in the hope that it would save them. His beloved fashioned more weapons from the sticks and stones at her feet, binding them together with strands of her hair. Together, they made their final stand, determined to protect their love at all costs.

But as their resources dwindled and with the angry tribespeople closing in, the lovers knew they faced a grim choice. They had to either surrender to a fate decreed by others or embrace the unknown depths of the ocean together. Clasping each other tightly, they chose the latter, stepping into the water. However, at that moment, when all seemed lost, the Great Spirit intervened. He was touched by the depth of their love and the courage of their defiance. The Great Spirit transformed the lovers into barramundi, granting them eternal life in the waters they had chosen as their escape.

Most barramundis are born male and eventually change to female, a mirror of the eternal bond between the man and woman, ensuring they would never be parted.

How the Cassowary Got Its Helmet

In Aboriginal culture, it is clear that the balance in the natural ecosystem is deeply respected, with each creature playing a vital role. However, the cassowary stands out as a leader and guardian of the rainforest. Cassowaries are recognized for their importance to the biodiversity of the Wet Tropics and Cape York. This majestic bird is also considered a prized food, with their feathers, claws, and bones valued for ornaments and tools.

Three species of cassowary.[25]

The story of how the cassowary got its helmet is a tale that portrays the bird's journey from an outcast to a respected member of the animal kingdom. It all began long ago in the lush, verdant expanses of the rainforest during a time when all beings lived in harmony. A young cassowary found himself the subject of relentless teasing due to his inability to fly. Isolated and saddened, he watched from the shadows as the other animals played in the water. He wanted to join, but he was worried about being teased.

One day, after the animals had left the swimming hole, the cassowary ventured out, hoping to enjoy a solitary swim and perhaps catch some fish for his dinner. However, his presence did not go unnoticed. A lizard spotted the cassowary hiding and called out to the others, mocking the bird for his flightlessness. The laughter that followed cut deep, and in his distress, the cassowary fled into the forest, crashing into a large rock with such force that a piece of stone became lodged in his head.

Embarrassed and hurt, the cassowary withdrew even further from the community, spending his days alone. One day, he encountered a seahawk, who offered him a new perspective.

"Hello there," the seahawk greeted the cassowary in a warm tone, surprising the bird. "What are you doing here all alone?"

"Well, I suppose being alone is better than being constantly teased by others," the cassowary replied. "They all make fun of my inability to fly, except you. I can't help but wonder why you're not teasing me like your friends do."

The seahawk smiled. He reassured the cassowary that he was different from the rest. He told the cassowary that everyone in this world has their own unique abilities and contributions. While the cassowary did not possess the ability to fly, he had other skills. The seahawk pointed out the cassowary's exceptional skills in fishing—the cassowary claimed he could easily catch fish in the river by spreading his wings, acting like a net—his talent for digging up yams with his claws, and, of course, his newfound strength that came with the stone helmet.

His moment of valor arrived the next day when the seahawk, injured by a group of attacking snakes, sought the cassowary's help. With courage fueled by his desire to protect his friend, the cassowary charged into the fray, using his powerful legs, sharp claws, and hard helmet to fend off the snakes.

From that day forth, the cassowary was no longer seen as a figure to mock. Instead, he was seen as a fearless leader and protector of the forest. The animals, who had once been quick to laugh, now looked at the cassowary with respect and gratitude, lifting him up as a hero.

This story, like many Dreamtime narratives, teaches the importance of recognizing and embracing one's unique qualities. It speaks to the importance of community, the strength found in diversity, and the role each being plays in maintaining the balance within the ecosystem.

To the Aboriginal people, natural elements are far more than resources for survival. They are imbued with spiritual significance, serving as totems that link individuals and communities to the land and its ancient stories. Rocks, rivers, plants, and animals are all honored as teachers and kin. A rock might embody the strength and endurance of the land, while a river may represent life's ever-flowing, ever-changing journey.

This holistic view of the world fosters a profound respect for the environment, teaching the importance of living in harmony with nature. It instills a sense of stewardship and a responsibility to care for the earth.

In Aboriginal cultures, every aspect of nature is a thread in the intricate web of life, each with its own story and significance. The natural world is a sacred space where the spiritual and physical realms merge.

Chapter 10: Spirits of the Outback

A lone man could be seen sitting by his campfire. It was dark, save for the glinting stars high up in the sky and the faint glow of the fire in front of him. Suddenly, his mind raced to the various stories he had heard about the Outback—the semi-arid inland areas of Australia that are typically remote—and the spirits that inhabited it. The man could feel his heart beating slightly faster as he recalled these stories, but he kept calm, reminding himself that they were nothing more than stories that served as warnings for wandering travelers like him to be cautious of their surroundings.

Indeed, it was just another calm night for the man until he heard an unsettling scraping sound breaking the stillness from somewhere nearby. His only reaction was to freeze; he dared not move a muscle. His gaze darted toward the dense line of trees where he thought the sound might have come from. His heart skipped a beat. Just beyond the reach of the firelight, the man saw a pair of eyes glinting with an unnatural glow. The figure emerged from the dark, its shadowed silhouette with long limbs immediately sending shivers down his spine.

The creature slowly approached, each of its steps making a rough, echoing scrape. This was because of its knees, which were encased in hard stone, knocked together as the creature walked. The man's terror grew as he saw a stone knife in one of the creature's hands. This sight confirmed his nightmare; the creature was none other than the Malingee.

According to Aboriginal mythology, Malingee is a rare and fearsome spirit that embodies the wild dangers of the night. The Malingee is especially familiar to the Aboriginal nations of the Northern Territory. The Malingee can be merciless when provoked, but it never seeks humans out for sport. It prefers to remain hidden, enjoying the silence of its domain. Yet, those who unwisely set up a campfire near its presence risk its wrath.

Interestingly, legend has it that the Malingee was not always a horrifying spirit of the night. Based on one version of the story, the spirit was once a man who wandered the land. Things changed when he crossed paths with a shaman. Details of this story are foggy, but the gist is that he somehow angered the shaman. As a punishment, he was transformed into a twisted creature, his humanity stripped away forever. There is no way to reverse the curse, and the man, now known as the Malingee, can only wander the Outback forever. He often hides within the dense forest or in caves, avoiding sunlight. Only when the sky turns dark does he emerge, occasionally targeting those who unconsciously disturb his domain.

Apart from the Malingee, the Outback is also the home of another spirit known as the Papinijuwari. Described as a giant with only a single eye, the Papinijuwari are believed to dwell in huts at the ends of the sky. This creature carries a torch whenever it sets out across the heavens. Its movement in the sky appears to human eyes as a shooting star.

In contrast to the Malingee, who do not typically seek humans, the Papinijuwari has an insatiable appetite. Drawn specifically to the scent of illness, the creature tracks down the sick. Once it has found its victim, the Papinijuwari drinks their blood. The terror does not stop there; the Papinijuwari then shrinks itself to a size small enough to enter the victim's body. Once inside, the spirit continues to feast, ultimately leading to the victim's death. Fortunately, sightings of Papinijuwari are rare. However, their presence is deeply feared—some might even consider the Papinijuwari to be one of the most dreaded spirits in Aboriginal folklore.

Moha Moha

Even the waters of Australia teem with mystery. The seas around the Great Barrier Reef hold their own collection of supernatural beings. One of them is named the Moha Moha.

Almost similar to the legend of the Loch Ness Monster, several sightings of Moha Moha have been reported. The first detailed account came from an unexpected witness in 1890, a schoolteacher named

Selina Lovell. The encounter took place on the shores of Great Sandy Island. Here, Lovell claimed to have witnessed the creature from only five feet away. For nearly half an hour, the schoolteacher watched the Moha Moha as it lingered in the shallows. It then turned and raised its body and tail above the water, revealing itself to the human for a short while before it slipped back into deeper waters, disappearing as suddenly as it had appeared.

Lovell described the creature vividly. It was nearly thirty feet long and had a massive dome-shaped body. Its serpentine neck, extending toward a saurian head, made the creature appear rather unsettling. The Moha Moha also had glossy skin, as if it were made of satin, while its head and neck were greenish-white. White spots dotted along its neck, and around its inky black eyes were a stark white band. Lovell claimed the Moha Moha had no visible nostrils but had serrated teeth. Because of this, many have concluded that it breathed through its mouth.

Perhaps the most peculiar feature of the creature is its greyish dome-shaped carapace, which spanned at least eight feet across and five feet high. The Moha Moha also sports a twelve-foot tail covered entirely in thumb-sized scales and has a brownish fin. Its head and tail apparently look like they come from different animals; some may even say the Moha Moha is almost similar to the Greek mythological creature the Chimera, which had different parts of animals attached to its body.

While the sighting must have left a lasting impression on Lovell, the Aboriginal people, especially those who called these coasts their home, were not at all surprised upon learning of this sighting. The Aboriginals view the Moha Moha as a coastal spirit who emerges from the sea every once in a while. However, this spirit is far from benevolent; once on land, it attacks camps and seizes unsuspecting people by the leg. These tales are popular among the Aboriginal nations because they serve as a warning of the ocean's hidden dangers.

Believe it or not, Lovell was not the only person to have reported a sighting of the Moha Moha. Captain James Cook claimed to have caught a glimpse of the spirit during his 1770 voyage. In the 1960s, another sighting was reported. This time around, it was by a fisherman named Jacob Lack. Instead of witnessing the spirit in the flesh, the fisherman was said to have come across its carcass decomposing on a rock.

Nadubi and Garkain

The Nadubi is well known among those on the rocky plateaus of Arnhem Land. According to the natives, the Nadubi is a spirit that often emerges in the chilly hours of the night. Its target is lone wanderers. At a single glance, the Nadubi might look like a human, but as one gets closer, there are a few fearsome distinctions that will terrify even the bravest. The spirit is often seen haunting the rugged terrain with sharp, barbed spines protruding from its elbows.

Ancient cave paintings across Arnhem Land captured the appearance of this spirit in detail. The painting in Gunbalanya, for instance, depicts Nadubi as a woman with spines sprouting not only from her elbows but also her lower body. Another mural at Sleisbeck pictures the Nadubi in a different form; the spirit was painted as a kangaroo-like figure with a spiny tail and barbed spines coming out from its mouth.

Legend has it that after silently stalking lone travelers, the Nadubi will attack them by projecting its barbed spines. They are lethal. The unsuspecting victims feel a slow and agonizing sickness creeping in as the spines pierce their flesh. They will eventually die unless the spines are swiftly removed. However, removing them is not an easy feat, and not everyone can do it. Only medicine men possess the knowledge to save these victims. Apart from having the skills to remove the lethal spines, these medicine men are also believed to have been gifted with a special sight, allowing them to detect the Nadubi's presence. However, the removal has to be done quickly; there are a lot of cases where help arrives too late.

While the Nadubi haunts the rugged plateaus, somewhere near the mouth of the Liverpool River dwells another solitary spirit. Known simply as the Garkain, this mysterious spirit also appears vaguely human in appearance. His biggest distinction is the large flaps of skin on his arms and legs, appearing similar to wings or massive fins. Because of this special feature, the Garkain has the ability to fly. He prefers to remain hidden during the day—he typically rests in silence beneath piles of leaves—but when the sky darkens, the spirit wreaks havoc, attacking anyone who trespasses into his territory.

To eliminate his victim, the Garkain first launches the individual into the air before swooping down upon them. Using his leathery flaps of skin, the spirit then wraps around the unfortunate traveler. Through this method, the spirit can suffocate his victims. This, however, is not the end of the traveler. The Garkain feasts on his victim. Since the spirit is tied deeply to his primal instincts—not knowing how to make fire or use tools—the Garkain often eats these wandering travelers raw.

The Yara-ma-yha-who, a Vampire-Like Creature

The legend about the Yara-ma-yha-who is one of the popular tales told to keep little ones safe. Parents often warn their children to steer away from giant fig trees scattered throughout the landscape, as this is where the Yara-ma-yha-who is said to wait for its next victim.

According to legend, the Yara-ma-yha-who has a rather small appearance. The spirit has a large head and oversized mouth. Apart from being red in color, the Yara-ma-yha-who's most striking feature is its fingers that end in tiny suction pads.

Since it often sits perched on branches of fig trees, the spirit can easily camouflage itself with the leaves and the branches. It will wait for hours for an unsuspecting traveler or a child to wander close to the tree where it dwells. The moment an individual approaches the tree, either to take a quick rest or even to seek shade, the Yara-ma-yha-who immediately seizes its opportunity. The spirit drops down without warning, clinging to its victim with its suction-cup fingers. Its grip is believed to be so strong that escape is nearly impossible. Then, the Yara-ma-yha-who proceeds to drink the blood of its struggling victim. However, unlike a typical vampire, the spirit never drains its victim completely. Instead, it drinks just enough to weaken them.

The spirit will leave its victim alone as it continues to stroll around, working up its appetite. With no strength, victims often find it extremely difficult to walk, let alone attempt an escape. They are left with no choice but to remain on the ground, waiting for the return of the spirit. When that moment comes, the Yara-ma-yha-who opens its mouth wide, almost like a hungry python, and swallows its victim headfirst, forcing them down into its belly. Once its prey is completely swallowed, the spirit stands upright and performs a rhythmic dance as if celebrating the feast.

Surprisingly, the horror does not stop there. After filling itself up, the spirit lays down, eventually drifting into a slumber. When it wakes, the Yara-ma-yha-who spits its victim out. Although still alive, the victim is no longer themself. According to the Aboriginal storyteller and writer David Unaipon, after their first encounter with the Yara-ma-yha-who, victims will find themselves shorter and weaker, with a hint of redness to their skin. If these same victims are unfortunate enough to cross paths with the spirit for a second time, they will grow even shorter, and their features will turn increasingly distorted. A third encounter is the worst of all; victims will transform into a Yara-ma-yha-who, cursed to turn into the very spirit that had harmed them.

Bunyip

The bunyip is known by many names. The Dharawal people of Australia's southeastern coast refer to the spirit as gu-ru-ngaty; the Wiradjuri people call it mirree-ulla. The Wemba-Wemba people call it banib and describe it as a mysterious creature that dwells in the waters along the Dhungala, or the Murray River. However, bunyip remains the most common name used to refer to the spirit.

Descriptions of the spirit vary significantly among Aboriginal nations. Some claim it appears as a half-human, half-fish creature with sharp fangs. It is also thought to possess eerie, mystical powers and has a chilling appetite for human flesh, especially innocent children. A bunyip can also let out echoing cries that inflict fear. It is also said to carry diseases such as rheumatism. Some agree that the bunyip is a shapeshifter; at times, it appears covered in shaggy fur, while other times, it appears coated in shiny scales and feathers. The spirit can also take the form of a dog, a massive cow, a seal-like creature, or even an emu. The colonial explorer George French Angas claimed that the spirit resembled a massive starfish.

The bunyip's origin also remains a topic of debate. Renowned paleontologists such as Pat Vickers-Rich and geologists like Neil Archbold proposed an intriguing theory regarding the origin of the spirit. These professionals suggest that the origin of the spirit traces back to sightings of the now-extinct *Diprotodon*, a giant herbivorous marsupial that once roamed Australia in ancient times. Early Aboriginal Australians inhabited the region alongside megafauna like *Diprotodon* for about twenty thousand years before these creatures went extinct. It could be plausible that stories of the bunyip evolved from sightings of this ancient animal.

Meanwhile, the Ngarrindjeri people of southeastern Australia claim that the legend of the bunyip—referred to as Mulyawonk by them—is born from a story about greed. The tale begins with a man who was beyond famished. Consumed by both hunger and greed, he caught more fish than he needed, thus depleting resources for others. To punish the greedy man, the elders cursed him, transforming half of the man's body into a fish-like creature. To this day, the Ngarrindjeri never fail to express caution that overfishing or environmental exploitation could awaken the bunyip, bringing misfortune upon those who show no respect for nature's balance.

Of course, the intriguing tales and descriptions of the mysterious bunyip caught the attention of many, including the European settlers when they arrived in Australia in the 18th century. Their curiosity peaked in 1846 when the world was surprised by news of the discovery of a peculiar skull unearthed in a tributary of the Murray River. Believed to be the remains of a bunyip, the skull was exhibited at Sydney's Australian Museum. However, this excitement was short-lived. After a careful scientific investigation, scholars revealed that the skull belonged not to the legendary water spirit but to a deformed horse.

The Terrorizing Whowie

Similar to the bunyip, the Whowie also dwells in the Murray River, particularly in the Riverina district of Australia. Resembling a giant goanna, the Whowie measures about twenty feet long and has six powerful legs that look like those belonging to a monitor lizard. Its head, however, resembles a frog, which makes its entire appearance both strange and frightening.

Despite having six powerful legs, the Whowie's movement is considered slow and deliberate. However, the spirit has little need for speed since its presence alone can send anyone who stumbles upon it fleeing in terror. When night comes, the Whowie can often be seen crawling into camps, sneaking in while people are deep asleep. The spirit captures anyone who is slow to escape and devours them whole. The Whowie is believed to have a mouth so massive that it can consume sixty people at one time. It is only when the sun begins to appear on the horizon that the Whowie retreats back to its cave on the Murray River. At times, the spirit can be seen basking along the riverbanks; some believe that the sandy hills of the Riverina were formed by the movement of this enormous spirit.

According to a legend passed down by the Aboriginals, there was a time when the Whowie went on a rampage. Its relentless attacks took a serious toll on the water-rat tribe that lived along the river. As desperation and fear grew, the tribe's chief thought it was high time for him to gather his people and discuss their dire situation. The chief eventually suggested that they abandon their home and make their way to safer lands. The people were saddened by this suggestion.

Suddenly, an elder stepped forward. He reminded the people of all the bountiful resources that their land had gifted them and the deep connection they had to the land. "We cannot lose hope now," the elder said. "Let us take another moment to think of other ways to rid this menace from our land."

Inspired by the words of the elder, the tribe agreed to stand their ground and end the threat of the Whowie once and for all. The water-rat tribe began to strategize. First, they set up night guards to watch over the people. Then, they summoned nearby tribes for assistance, hoping that by working together, they could at least drive away the spirit. This call for arms was a success; tribes from all over the land, including the kangaroo, platypus, eagle, magpie, cockatoo, lizard, snake, opossum, and crow tribes, came to lend their strength. Together, the people held a great corroboree, where they spent the night dancing and telling stories. It was only when dawn came that they made a move to find the Whowie.

After following tracks and traces left behind by the Whowie, the people successfully found its lair; it was a cave with only a single entrance. The cave was believed to be so vast that it would take the Whowie nearly a week to crawl out. The people prepared their trap. They first gathered massive piles of sticks and branches before bundling them into heaps. They arranged the wood halfway inside the cave and at its entrance, creating a barricade of fuel for their fire.

After a while, scouts came back, reporting that the Whowie was about to emerge. With haste, they set the wood ablaze, causing thick smoke and flames to fill the cave. A roar pierced the air, as the Whowie found itself trapped inside its very own shelter. The spirit could do nothing; it was helpless against the choking smoke. It struggled through the narrow passages for six days. Blinded and suffocating from the thick smoke, the Whowie grew more and more desperate to reach the exit. It eventually reached the mouth of the cave on the seventh day, though it was barely alive; it was already burned and desperately gasping for air.

Seizing the opportunity, the tribes immediately launched their attack. With their spears, axes, and nulla-nullas (a type of hardwood club used by the Aborigines), they laid blows on the giant goanna. No longer able to defend itself, the Whowie, which was already mortally wounded, dragged itself back into the cave. The tribes never saw the spirit again.

However, many believe that the Whowie still remains in the cave. Its sigh can sometimes be heard from the cave on the Murray River. Although the giant lizard is no longer a threat to the tribes, his legend continues to be remembered and feared. Elders warn lone travelers of such a spirit in the wilds, and parents often warn their children with tales of the Whowie, urging them to behave unless they want the spirit to emerge from his cave and wreak terror once more.

Chapter 11: Aboriginal Warriors Who Fought for Their Lands

The year was 1783, and Britain had just lost its grip on its American colonies. The blow left the empire scrambling for solutions to new and pressing problems. In the wake of the American Revolutionary War, the jails of England swelled with inmates, a result of ending the practice of transporting convicts to the American colonies. Desperate for an alternative, the British government turned its eyes to a distant land that had already been claimed for the British Crown by James Cook: Australia.

A depiction of Cook's landing at Botany Bay, located in Sydney.[26]

The convicts destined for transportation were a diverse lot, with the majority of their crimes considered minor in today's justice systems. Many were guilty of petty theft, a crime often born out of necessity rather than malice. The majority of these convicts hailed from England's teeming industrial cities, showing the widespread poverty and desperation that plagued the lower classes. Another small portion came from Ireland, and an even smaller number hailed from Scotland and Wales.

The solution to England's overcrowded jails materialized in the form of the First Fleet. This was an armada of eleven ships commanded by Captain Arthur Phillip, a highly experienced British naval officer tasked with founding a penal colony in an uncharted territory. Under Phillip's leadership, the fleet eventually reached the shores of what is now known as Circular Quay. On January 26th, 1788, they established a convict settlement at Sydney Cove. This date marked the beginning of convict settlements in Australia, a monumental event that would forever change the trajectory of the land and its people.

Of course, setting up a new settlement was anything but a walk in the park. The colony immediately grappled with the threat of starvation. The seeds they had brought all the way from England either spoiled or failed to grow in the Australian soil. The weather was completely different, and the majority of people knew nothing about farming the land.

Captain Phillip knew he must do everything he could to ensure the survival of the colony. He first insisted that what little food there was had to be shared equally among convicts and free settlers. This decision, along with his policy of granting land to convicts he deemed trustworthy, drew ire from the British officers. Yet, these policies allowed the colony to survive.

The landing of the First Fleet in Port Jackson, 1788.[27]

However, despite their efforts to make the colony work, the British soon realized they faced another challenge, one that was far bigger than the struggles of establishing farms or managing dissent. The colonizers were about to meet the Aboriginal warriors, the original inhabitants and traditional custodians of the vast land. The warriors were strong fighters and determined to protect their homes.

So, now we turn our attention to Pemulwuy, an Aboriginal warrior whose bravery and fight against the foreign settlers marked a significant chapter in Australian history.

Pemulwuy: The Fearless Bidjigal Warrior

Pemulwuy's story begins in the heartland of the Bidjigal clan, which is part of the broader Eora nation that originally inhabited what is now known as Sydney. The British settlers were made aware of Pemulwuy's existence as early as October 1790, thanks to Bennelong, an Aboriginal man who had forged a relationship with the colonizers. Bennelong, who had been captured by Governor Arthur Phillip but later became an intermediary between the British and Aboriginal people, mentioned Pemulwuy to the foreigners. It is still uncertain whether Bennelong's intention was to warn the British about Pemulwuy specifically or if there were other reasons behind his mentioning the warrior. However, as an intermediary, it makes sense for Bennelong to share information about significant figures within the Aboriginal communities (by this time,

Pemulwuy had already displayed signs of resistance against the British encroachment).

Pemulwuy was also known to be a *carradhy*, or a clever man, as he possessed abilities that went beyond the ordinary, including healing wounds. Colebee, a Cadigal headman, informed Governor Phillip that Pemulwuy could be easily recognized by an injury to the toes of his left foot, which had been caused by a club. This detail fascinated many, as anthropologists have observed similar customs among the kadaicha men of Central Australia (spiritual enforcers who carry out justice or punishments within the community according to traditional law), who would dislocate their small toes to move quickly and quietly. There were even stories that Pemulwuy could transform himself into a bird to flee from danger.

An illustration of Pemulwuy in his canoe.[38]

The first major conflict between Pemulwuy and the British occurred on December 10th, 1790, and involved the spearing of John McIntyre, Governor Phillip's gamekeeper. This incident was not just a random act of violence but also a calculated response to the tensions simmering between the Aboriginal people and the settlers. On that day, McIntyre was resting in a hide with a hunting party near Cooks River when they heard noises from the bush. Investigating the sounds, they saw four Aboriginal men, including Pemulwuy, stealthily approaching.

McIntyre believed he recognized the men and halted his party from attacking. He attempted to communicate with the Aboriginals, offering them bread as a gesture of peace. However, when he laid down his gun, Pemulwuy stepped onto a log, positioned his spear on his *woomera* (spear thrower), and launched it toward McIntyre. The spear, tipped with jagged silcrete flakes, struck McIntyre, piercing deep and perforating his lung. When the surgeon, John White, later removed the spearhead, he found it barbed with small pieces of red stone, a design meant to ensure it inflicted maximum damage.

Bennelong's Dual Loyalties

Upon the arrival of the British, the Eora people deliberately avoided contact. Governor Arthur Phillip was eager to understand the language and customs of the local population, so he resorted to a desperate measure: kidnapping. On November 25th, 1789, Bennelong and Colebee were captured as part of Phillip's plan. Once, Bennelong speared Phillip during a whale feast organized by the British to mend relations with the Eora. Despite this aggressive encounter, Phillip and Bennelong eventually reestablished their complicated relationship. Bennelong was even exposed to European culture and taken to England sometime in 1792. However, he returned to Australia three years later, only to find that his people were still experiencing even more hardship under British rule.

In hindsight, evidence suggests that Bennelong and Colebee might have indirectly collaborated with Pemulwuy in the spearing of John McIntyre. McIntyre was known for carrying a musket and competing with the Indigenous population for food. Bennelong deeply resented him. McIntyre trespassed on Bidjigal land, hunting animals that were considered totemic spirit ancestors by the local people, such as possums, kangaroos, emus, and dingoes. McIntyre was also suspected of having harmed or even killed several Aboriginal individuals during his hunting expeditions; some accounts even state that he admitted to shooting an Aboriginal man.

McIntyre survived the initial attack but succumbed to his wounds on January 20th, 1791. The incident shocked the settlement, as many believed the attack was unprovoked. After all, McIntyre had been unarmed at the time. Governor Phillip was convinced of the need for retribution and to assert control. He ordered a punitive expedition led by Captain Watkin Tench.

Perhaps consumed by his bloodthirst, Phillip demanded the capture of two Bidjigal men and ordered Tench to behead ten more. However, recognizing the brutality of such orders, Captain Watkin Tench proposed a less bloodthirsty plan. He suggested capturing six Bidjigal and bringing them to Sydney Cove, insisting that none should be killed outright. Phillip accepted Tench's proposal, and the expedition set out on December 14th, marking the largest military operation since the colony's founding. Despite their efforts, after three days of searching, there was no trace of Pemulwuy or the Bidjigal. On December 17th, Tench called for a retreat to Sydney Cove to regroup and resupply.

The resistance was just beginning, though. Pemulwuy persuaded the Eora, Dharug, and Tharawal people to join his campaign against the settlers. From 1792 onward, this formidable warrior led numerous raids on British colonists, striking at various sites and demonstrating his courage and strategic acumen.

In December 1795, Pemulwuy and his warriors launched an attack on a work party at Botany Bay, which included "Black Caesar," an early settler of African descent and a renowned bushranger (a term referring to outlaws in colonial Australia). Caesar managed to crack Pemulwuy's skull in the skirmish. Many believed this blow would be fatal, but Pemulwuy survived, cementing his legend and the belief in his near-immortality.

March 1797 saw Pemulwuy leading a daring raid against a government farm at Toongabbie. After a series of raids near Parramatta, a group of armed settlers and soldiers clashed with over one hundred Aboriginal warriors at dawn. The punitive party, tired of the chase, entered the town, only to be followed by Pemulwuy and a large group of warriors. Pemulwuy speared a soldier, sparking a battle. The settlers' first volley of gunfire killed at least five Aboriginal warriors. Pemulwuy was severely wounded, with seven buckshot wounds to his head and body.

Despite the severity of his injuries, Pemulwuy's capture did not spell the end of him. Held in custody at a Parramatta hospital, still filled with buckshot and shackled with a leg iron, he managed an astounding escape.

The Battle of Parramatta elevated Pemulwuy's stature among the Aboriginal people as an invincible figure. He was revered as the mastermind behind subsequent raids on British farms for food. However, his injuries limited his capabilities, leading to a diminished resistance effort in his final years.

On November 22nd, 1801, Governor Philip Gidley King issued a proclamation for Pemulwuy's capture, offering a reward for him, dead or alive. Then, in early June 1802, Pemulwuy's life came to an end at the hands of Henry Hacking, the first mate of the Royal Navy ship *Lady Nelson*.

Yet, the spirit and strength of the Aboriginal people did not end with Pemulwuy. Instead, his legacy ignited an even greater flame of resistance. Pemulwuy's son, Tedbury, took up his father's cause. He fought valiantly for several more years before his own death in 1810. Through their courageous efforts, the legacy of resistance and the indomitable spirit of the Aboriginal people lived on, proving their enduring fight for their land, culture, and rights.

Jandamarra: The Bunuba Resistance Leader

Born in the 1870s into the Bunuba tribe, Jandamarra's early years were marked by a unique bridging of worlds. The Bunuba people, known for their deep connection to the mountainous Kimberley region of Western Australia, faced the encroachment of European settlers with a mix of resistance and adaptation. At about the age of eleven, Jandamarra and his mother stepped away from the traditional life to settle at Lennard River Station, one of the earliest pastoral stations in the Kimberley. This decision marked the beginning of Jandamarra's complex relationship with the European world.

Under the expansive skies of the Kimberley and the watchful eyes of the settlers, Jandamarra quickly mastered skills that were alien to his people but essential for survival in a changing world. He became adept at riding horses, shearing sheep, and using firearms. His proficiency in these areas, coupled with his exceptional physical agility—despite his small stature, Jandamarra was swift—earned him the nickname "Pigeon" from William Lukin, the owner of the River Station. Jandamarra's ability to speak English fluently and confidently set him apart.

However, despite his early assimilation into station life, the call of his ancestral lands was strong. At the age of fifteen, Jandamarra returned to his traditional lands for initiation into Bunuba law, a rite of passage that reconnected him with his roots. He started to hone his hunting skills, blending his newfound talents with the traditional knowledge passed down through generations.

In 1889, a pivotal moment occurred when Jandamarra and a fellow tribesman—some said he was also Jandamarra's uncle—known as Ellemarra were captured by police at Windjina Gorge. They were accused of killing sheep. The two men were chained together and forced to march to Derby, where they were to be charged. After a period of incarceration, Jandamarra's charges were unexpectedly dropped. He was offered freedom in exchange for his services in caring for police horses.

About a year later, Jandamarra returned to Lennard River as a stockman. However, this was nothing more than a brief return. Perhaps hearing a whisper of calling from his ancestors, Jandamarra returned to his traditional land. He soon found himself in conflict with Bunuba law; since he worked for the settlers, he was seen as betraying his duty to protect his people's lands.

Hoping to avoid retribution, Jandamarra escaped and left his home yet again. Seeking refuge, he arrived at Lillimooloora Station, where fate introduced him to Bill Richardson, a stockman turned police officer. Richardson recognized Jandamarra's skills and, perhaps understanding the value of his knowledge of the land and people, employed him as a tracker. As an Aboriginal tracker, Jandamarra's duties were to assist the police in tracking down Aboriginal people who had a reputation for strongly resisting the settlers' encroachment on their land. Sometimes, these people were also tracked down simply for occupying or using land that settlers now claimed as their own. These targeted Aborigines often ended up getting removed from their land, never to be seen by their tribe or family again.

Together, Jandamarra and Richardson made a formidable team. They set a standard for effectiveness in tracking down those who sought refuge in the vast and rugged terrain of the Kimberley. Jandamarra and Richardson eventually developed a close relationship. There was also a time when Jandamarra saved Richardson's life from an assault launched by the Aborigines. However, this partnership put Jandamarra in a unique position. He was tracking down his own people, using the very skills that tied him to his culture and ancestors. Jandamarra navigated a delicate balance between survival and betrayal.

The work Jandamarra and Richardson undertook together was a source of deep inner turmoil for Jandamarra. He was torn between the loyalty he felt for his companion and the duty he owed to his people. Some sources claim that this period of Jandamarra's life was also marred by personal controversies. Allegations of reckless behavior, particularly in flouting kinship and skin laws, surfaced, complicating his standing within the Bunuba community.

However, Jandamarra soon realized that his ties with his people were stronger than he ever imagined. The settlers' livestock were frequently stolen or speared by Aboriginal people, a form of resistance against the invasion and the use of their lands. In response, the Europeans tasked Jandamarra with capturing a group of Bunuba men responsible for these actions at Lillimooloora Station. Upon successfully capturing the group, Jandamarra was immediately confronted with the reality of his actions. Among the captured group were not only the most senior Bunuba leaders and elders but also Ellemarra and a few of his own bloodline. They confronted Jandamarra.

"Look around you," Ellemarra said to him. "I raised you, yet look at what you have done to us."

Jandamarra felt a surge of guilt after being reminded of his obligations to his own people. The Bunuba also spoke of a new policeman at Fitzroy Crossing who had been recklessly killing Aboriginal people, further igniting Jandamarra's sense of duty to his community.

In a moment of defiance, Jandamarra shot and killed Richardson as he slept. He then armed his people, rallying a group of warriors to ambush the Europeans. On November 10th, 1894, this armed gang attacked five white men driving cattle through Bunuba land, killing two and seizing their weapons. This act of rebellion was a declaration of war against the European settlers and marked a significant escalation in the conflict.

The most famous battle under Jandamarra's leadership occurred in 1894 at Windjana Gorge. A fierce confrontation unfolded between fifty Bunuba warriors and thirty police officers. In the heat of battle, Ellemarra was killed, and Jandamarra was terribly wounded, yet he managed to escape. His miraculous recovery only added to his legendary status, instilling fear in the police across the state for his exceptional shooting skills and intimate knowledge of the land.

The growing retaliation led John Forrest, Western Australia's first premier, to order a crackdown on the rebellion. Police attacks on camps around Fitzroy Crossing resulted in the deaths of several Aboriginal people. They were killed purely on suspicion of having ties to Jandamarra's resistance band.

For the next three years, Jandamarra led a guerrilla war against the police and European settlers, employing hit-and-run tactics and vanishing acts that became the stuff of legends. One famous incident involved a police patrol tracking him to his hideout at Tunnel Creek's entrance, only for Jandamarra to disappear mysteriously through the tunnel system within the mountains.

Jandamarra's end came at the hands of another Aboriginal tracker, Micki or Minko Mick, who was reputed to possess magical powers. On April 1st, 1897, Mick tracked Jandamarra down and shot him dead at Tunnel Creek. The white troopers decapitated Jandamarra as proof of his demise, and his head was sent to a firearms company in England to showcase the "effectiveness" of their weapons. His family buried his body in the Napier Range, placing it inside a boab tree.

It has been over a century since his death, yet Jandamarra's legacy is still alive. His story is remembered in stories, dances, and songs, both traditional and contemporary. His legend was of a tragic hero caught between two worlds. Jandamarra's story was one of the most dramatic tales of the 19th-century conflict between Aboriginal people and white settlers, highlighting the complexities of identity, resistance, and the enduring spirit of the Aboriginal people.

Conclusion

We have journeyed across the expanse of Australia's heartlands, delved into the depths of its oldest stories, and discovered the wisdom of the world's most ancient natural wonders. These stories are not outdated tales. They are the voices of the ancestors, speaking of the creation, the land, and the laws that have guided Aboriginal peoples for tens of thousands of years. The importance of preserving these narratives cannot be overstated; they are a bridge to understanding the past, a guide for the present, and a legacy for the future.

Embedded within these tales are important moral lessons that resonate deeply with contemporary issues. Take, for instance, the story of Tiddalik the frog, who drank all the water in the world, causing a great drought. This tale warns of the dangers of greed and the importance of considering the needs of others, reflecting on our modern-day challenges of resource depletion and environmental sustainability. The legend of Gulaga Mountain teaches us about the deep connection between the land and life, reminding us of the nurturing role nature plays and our duty to protect and honor our natural world.

The stories of courageous fighters like Jandamarra and Pemulwuy, who resisted colonial forces to protect their land, revolve around the themes of resistance, resilience, and the fight for justice. These tales celebrate the heroic deeds of these figures and also underscore the value of standing up for one's rights and the protection of sacred lands.

By keeping these stories alive, we honor the legacy of those who have gone before us and offer a gift of knowledge and understanding to those who come after us. This is not just a responsibility that belongs to historians and scholars alone; it is a call to all of us to listen, learn, and share. Whether through books, storytelling, or digital media, efforts to preserve and share these stories are a step toward a richer, more connected world. It is about giving voice to the wisdom that has too often been overlooked yet has so much to offer in our search for a sustainable way to live on this planet.

Here's another book by Enthralling History that you might like

Free limited time bonus

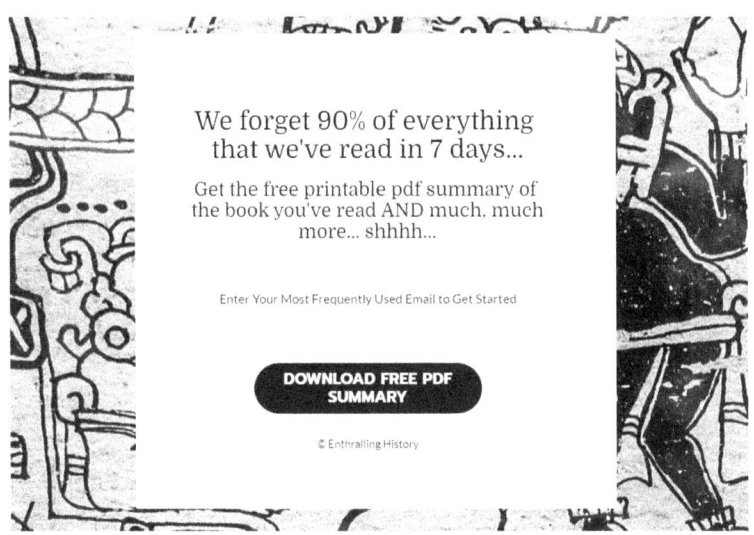

Stop for a moment. We have a free bonus set up for you. The problem is this: we forget 90% of everything that we read after 7 days. Crazy fact, right? Here's the solution: we've created a printable, 1-page pdf summary for this book that you're reading now. All you have to do to get your free pdf summary is to go to the following website: https://livetolearn.lpages.co/enthrallinghistory/

Or, Scan the QR code!

Once you do, it will be intuitive. Enjoy, and thank you!

Bibliography

ABC News. (2018, August 18). My beloved Great Barrier Reef: Four tales of love, loss and hope. *ABC News*. https://amp.abc.net.au/article/9748398

Aboriginal belief and story. (n.d.). Flightless Birds. https://infoflightlessbirdshelp.weebly.com/aboriginal-belief-and-story.html

Australian Aboriginal Myths & Legends. (n.d.). https://members.optusnet.com.au/virgothomas/space/abobeliefs2.html

Bernheimer, K., Bernheimer, A., & Snøhetta. (2016). Fairy Tale Architecture: Tiddalik The Frog. *Places-a Forum of Environmental Design, 2016*. https://doi.org/10.22269/161219

Biography - Jandamarra - Indigenous Australia. (n.d.). https://ia.anu.edu.au/biography/jandamarra-8822

Bohra The Kangaroo. (n.d.). www.kullillaart.com.au. https://www.kullillaart.com.au/dreamtime-stories/Bohra-The-Kangaroo

Death and Sorry business | Common ground. (n.d.). https://www.commonground.org.au/article/death-and-sorry-business

Dreamtime Stories: The Turtle. (2020, August 13). Yarn Marketplace. https://www.yarn.com.au/blogs/yarn-in-the-community/dreamtime-stories-the-turtle

Dreamtime Story: The Seven Sisters. (2020, December 8). Yarn Marketplace. https://www.yarn.com.au/blogs/yarn-in-the-community/dreamtime-story-the-seven-sisters

Gariwerd/Grampians - Budja Budja Aboriginal Cooperative. (2018, April 4). Budja Budja Aboriginal Cooperative. https://budjabudjacoop.org.au/about/gariwerdgrampians/

Hamilton, J. (2020, October 7). Seven Sisters stars creation story reconnecting people to their country after clifftop massacre taboo lifted. *ABC News.* https://www.abc.net.au/news/2020-10-08/wirangu-seven-sisters-songline-indigenous-healing-reconciliation/12380698

How the Sun was made. (n.d.). www.kullillaart.com.au. https://www.kullillaart.com.au/dreamtime-stories/How-the-Sun-was-made

Japingka Aboriginal Art. (2022, January 31). *Rainbow Serpent Dreamtime Story - Japingka Aboriginal Art Gallery.* Japingka Aboriginal Art Gallery. https://japingkaaboriginalart.com/articles/rainbow-serpent/#:~:text=Rainbow%20Serpent%20Rituals&text=They%20will%20sing%20out%20the,no%20harm%20or%20ill%20doing

Japingka Aboriginal Art. (2023, October 18). *Seven Sisters (Pleiades) star Dreaming Story - Aboriginal art stories.* Japingka Aboriginal Art Gallery. https://japingkaaboriginalart.com/articles/star-dreaming-seven-sisters/

Kangaroo Totem and Dreamtime Stories. (2020, July 24). Yarn Marketplace. https://www.yarn.com.au/blogs/yarn-in-the-community/kangaroo-totem-and-dreamtime-stories

National Theatre of Scotland. (2016, October 12). *Sharing a story through Aboriginal Australian Songline* [Video]. YouTube. https://www.youtube.com/watch?v=QYziHh98AC8

Paul Taylor. (2015, March 12). *Gujingga Songline* [Video]. YouTube. https://www.youtube.com/watch?v=oZGu7z2-XEU

Pemulwuy | The Dictionary of Sydney. (n.d.). https://dictionaryofsydney.org/entry/pemulwuy

Reynolds, P. (n.d.). *An Anangu story.* https://home.philreynolds.org.uk/travel/story.php

Songlines: Seven Sisters Tree Women and Wati Nyiru | The Box, Plymouth. (n.d.). The Box Plymouth. https://www.theboxplymouth.com/blog/art/songlines-tree-women

Stories in the stars. (n.d.). Museums Victoria. https://museumsvictoria.com.au/learning/little-science/teacher-support-materials/stories-in-the-stars/

Sydney Opera House. (2016, May 28). *Songlines explained: A 360 experience with Rhoda Roberts* [Video]. YouTube. https://www.youtube.com/watch?v=33O08xrQpR8

The birth of the Butterflies. (n.d.). www.kullillaart.com.au. https://www.kullillaart.com.au/dreamtime-stories/The-Birth-of-the-Butterflies

The First Fleet arrives at Sydney Cove | Australia's Defining Moments Digital Classroom | National Museum of Australia. (n.d.). https://digital-classroom.nma.gov.au/defining-moments/first-fleet-arrives-sydney-cove

The Guardian. (2019, December 7). *A healing corroboree at the foothills of Mount Gulaga, on Yuin country - in pictures.*
https://www.theguardian.com/australia-news/gallery/2019/dec/08/a-healing-corroboree-at-the-foothills-of-mount-gulaga-on-yuin-country-in-pictures.

The Lungkata story. (n.d.). Uluru-Kata Tjuta National Park.
https://parksaustralia.gov.au/uluru/discover/culture/stories/lungkata-story/#:~:text=The%20western%20face%20of%20Uluru,traditional%20management%20of%20the%20land

The Rainbow Serpent | Common ground. (n.d.).
https://www.commonground.org.au/bedtime-stories/the-rainbow-serpent

The Rainbow Serpent Dreamtime Story | Kate Owen Gallery. (n.d.).
https://www.kateowengallery.com/page/rainbow-serpent#:~:text=Two%20brothers%2C%20known%20as%20the,Instead%2C%20he%20swallowed%20them%20whole

The Southern Cross. (n.d.). www.kullillaart.com.au.
https://www.kullillaart.com.au/dreamtime-stories/The-Southern-Cross-Yaraandoo-The-place-of-the-white-gum-tree

Vij, R. (2022, February 3). *Story from Australia: How the Kangaroo Got its Tail & Wombat its Flat-head?* NutSpace. https://nutspace.in/how-kangaroo-got-tail-wombat-flat-head/

Wikipedia contributors. (2024, February 13). *Australian Aboriginal religion and mythology.* Wikipedia.
https://en.wikipedia.org/wiki/Australian_Aboriginal_religion_and_mythology#cite_note-FOOTNOTEBird_Rose2003163%E2%80%93168-34

Willis, L. (2022, February 2). *Returning to Country brings wellbeing.* Reconciliation Australia. https://www.reconciliation.org.au/returning-to-country-brings-wellbeing/

Image Sources

[1] NordNordWest, CC BY 3.0 <https://creativecommons.org/licenses/by/3.0>, via Wikimedia Commons: https://commons.wikimedia.org/wiki/File:Aboriginal_regions.png

[2] Faithy05, CC BY-SA 3.0 <http://creativecommons.org/licenses/by-sa/3.0/>, via Wikimedia Commons: https://commons.wikimedia.org/wiki/File:Biamie%27s_Cave.jpg

[3] Faithy05 at the English Wikipedia, CC BY-SA 3.0 <http://creativecommons.org/licenses/by-sa/3.0/>, via Wikimedia Commons: https://commons.wikimedia.org/wiki/File:Mt_Yengo.jpg

[4] Ek2030372672, CC BY-SA 4.0 <https://creativecommons.org/licenses/by-sa/4.0>, via Wikimedia Commons: https://commons.wikimedia.org/wiki/File:ULURU.jpg

[5] https://commons.wikimedia.org/wiki/File:Pleiades_Deep_dive.jpg

[6] Starnutoditopo, CC BY-SA 4.0 <https://creativecommons.org/licenses/by-sa/4.0>, via Wikimedia Commons: https://commons.wikimedia.org/wiki/File:Seven_Sisters_coin_Royal_Australian_Mint_1_dollar_2020_Reverse.jpg

[7] The original uploader was Digitaltribes at English Wikipedia., CC BY 2.5 <https://creativecommons.org/licenses/by/2.5>, via Wikimedia Commons: https://commons.wikimedia.org/wiki/File:RainbowSerpent.jpg

[8] Nick-D, CC BY-SA 3.0 <https://creativecommons.org/licenses/by-sa/3.0>, via Wikimedia Commons: https://commons.wikimedia.org/wiki/File:Gosses_Bluff_crater_from_the_air_April_2014.jpg

[9] Till Credner, CC BY-SA 3.0 <https://creativecommons.org/licenses/by-sa/3.0>, via Wikimedia Commons: https://commons.wikimedia.org/wiki/File:Constellation_Corona_Australis.jpg

[10] Dylan O'Donnell, deography.com, CC0, via Wikimedia Commons: https://commons.wikimedia.org/wiki/File:M45_The_Pleiades_Seven_Sisters.jpg

[11] Till Credner, CC BY-SA 3.0 <https://creativecommons.org/licenses/by-sa/3.0>, via Wikimedia Commons: https://commons.wikimedia.org/wiki/File:BootesCC.jpg

[12] Till Credner, CC BY-SA 3.0 <https://creativecommons.org/licenses/by-sa/3.0>, via Wikimedia Commons: https://commons.wikimedia.org/wiki/File:Constellation_Crux.jpg

[13] *PotMart186, CC BY-SA 4.0 <https://creativecommons.org/licenses/by-sa/4.0/>, via Wikimedia Commons: https://commons.wikimedia.org/wiki/File:Red_Kangaroos_at_Sturt_National_Park_NSW.jpg*

[14] *PanBK at the English-language Wikipedia, CC BY-SA 3.0 <http://creativecommons.org/licenses/by-sa/3.0/>, via Wikimedia Commons: https://commons.wikimedia.org/wiki/File:Wombat-Narawntapu.jpg*

[15] *Kpravin2, CC BY-SA 4.0 <https://creativecommons.org/licenses/by-sa/4.0>, via Wikimedia Commons: https://commons.wikimedia.org/wiki/File:Byron_Bay_Lighthouse,_Beach_and_Hinterland_in_the_Northern_Rivers,_NSW,_Australia.jpg*

[16] *I, Thierry Caro, CC BY-SA 3.0 <http://creativecommons.org/licenses/by-sa/3.0/>, via Wikimedia Commons: https://commons.wikimedia.org/wiki/File:Eretmochelys-imbricata-K%C3%A9lonia-2.JPG*

[17] *JJ Harrison (https://tiny.jjharrison.com.au/t/ZoQvcc0.5qhmjQ9eE), CC BY-SA 4.0 <https://creativecommons.org/licenses/by-sa/4.0/>, via Wikimedia Commons: https://commons.wikimedia.org/wiki/File:Corvus_coronoides_-_Doughboy_Head.jpg*

[18] *Ed Dunens, CC BY 2.0 <https://creativecommons.org/licenses/by/2.0>, via Wikimedia Commons: https://commons.wikimedia.org/wiki/File:Wedge-tailed_Eagle_(35713410886).jpg*

[19] *JJ Harrison (https://www.jjharrison.com.au/), CC BY-SA 3.0 <https://creativecommons.org/licenses/by-sa/3.0>, via Wikimedia Commons: https://commons.wikimedia.org/wiki/File:Dacelo_novaeguineae_waterworks.jpg*

[20] *en:User:Tnarg 12345, CC BY-SA 3.0 <http://creativecommons.org/licenses/by-sa/3.0/>, via Wikimedia Commons: https://commons.wikimedia.org/wiki/File:Cyclorana_platycephala.jpg*

[21] *JJ Harrison (https://www.jjharrison.com.au/), CC BY-SA 3.0 <https://creativecommons.org/licenses/by-sa/3.0>, via Wikimedia Commons: https://commons.wikimedia.org/wiki/File:Tiliqua_scincoides_scincoides.jpg*

[22] *Ayanadak123, CC BY-SA 4.0 <https://creativecommons.org/licenses/by-sa/4.0>, via Wikimedia Commons: https://commons.wikimedia.org/wiki/File:The_dazzling_colours_of_the_Great_Barrier_Reef_near_Airlie_Beach,_Whitsunday_Islands,_Queensland.jpg*

[23] *https://commons.wikimedia.org/wiki/File:Bermagui_Beach_01.JPG*

[24] *Mitch Ames, CC BY-SA 4.0 <https://creativecommons.org/licenses/by-sa/4.0>, via Wikimedia Commons: https://commons.wikimedia.org/wiki/File:Lates_calcarifer_2014-09-19a.jpg*

[25] *PaleoNeolitic (montage creator)BS Thurner HofKora27Martin Sordilla, CC BY-SA 3.0 <https://creativecommons.org/licenses/by-sa/3.0/>, via Wikimedia Commons: https://commons.wikimedia.org/wiki/File:Cassowary_Diversity.jpg*

[26] *https://commons.wikimedia.org/wiki/File:Cook%27s_landing_at_Botany_Bay.jpg*

[27] *https://commons.wikimedia.org/wiki/File:The_First_Fleet_entering_Port_Jackson,_January_26,_1788,_drawn_1888_A9333001h.jpg*

[28] *https://commons.wikimedia.org/wiki/File:Pemulwuy_aka_Pimbloy.jpg*